A.J. BEAMAN
39 PIMBO ROAD

39 PIMBO ROAD

# MEMORIES OF LNER STEAM

# MEMORIES OF LNER STEAM

## Raymond Keeley

LONDON

IAN ALLAN LTD

First published 1980

ISBN 0 7110 1038 2

Published by Ian Allan Ltd, Shepperton, Surrey;
and printed by Ian Allan Printing Ltd at their works
at Coombelands in Runnymede, England

# Contents

# Introduction

The steam locomotive was a remarkable machine and not least among its attributes was longevity. During the period 1950-60, when I was active with a camera, steam dominated, all modern classes of LNER engines still being at work, supported by a surprisingly large number of veterans from pre-Grouping days, some being of great age. They were like old soldiers who never die and, no doubt due to their simple robust construction, the fading away was a very slow process.

According to those among us who considered ourselves knowledgable, both footplate experts and the armchair amateurs, some of the older engines were better performers than the more modern types supposed to replace them. But the pre-Grouping engines usually looked their age and doubtless were part of an image successive railway boards wished to eliminate. To the lover of railways and locomotives their presence was a constant joy and their passing a source of accumulating heartache for, unlike our Victorian or Edwardian stations, bridges, viaducts, signalboxes etc, many of which remain in use, the locomotives and carriages of the period have, with the exception of a handful of preserved specimens, gone for scrap.

This book provides an opportunity to bring out long concealed prints, from my own camera and that of my friend Alan Blencowe. Herein you will find elite express locomotives, suburban tanks and humble goods, in stations, on shed and at locations sometimes unfamiliar in print. Pictures of, for example, the 'Directors' in their last golden summer at Sheffield and the Λ5 4-6-2Ts at Manchester, do not often appear. I hope my selection makes some amends.

The taking of the photographs often involved early rising and sometimes anguished moments when sun hid behind cloud at a vital time, or swirling smoke and steam blurred that which you wished to be seen. Some of the prints are in one way or another technically imperfect, in these cases an interesting or evocative picture has taken precedence over the pin sharp print.

I have divided the book into a number of sections or, if you like, essays, each with a relevant collection of photographs. My hope is that you will find the writing evocative — you may even find it provocative! At least I hope it succeeds in being a stimulant to the pictures.

Finally I wish to acknowledge the debt I owe my old friend Alan Blencowe for the freely given access I have had to his treasure store of photographs. Also to my wife who painted, decorated, gardened, that I may be free to write and type. Last but not least to my non railway enthusiast friend Kenneth Challinor who listened and advised, even though claiming to know not the difference between smokebox and firebox!

Stockport
Cheshire

*Raymond Keeley*

# LNER Pacifics:

## Reflections on men and machines

Pacific! The word has a magic ring, a name that brings a profusion of exciting images to the mind's eye of those immersed in the world of railways. Between them the Gresley, Stanier and Bulleid Pacifics possessed a greater share of legend and fame than any other grouping of locomotives. These mercurial ever young engines and their exploits provide a talking point wherever enthusiasts gather. The names, the legends, true and imaginary, polished, burnished anew, forever to glow in the affections of men who love steam locomotives. Respective merits will be debated, defended, argued, *Mallard* and 126mph will come in one breath, claims for the 'Duchesses' flattening Shap long before the electrics came off the drawing board will be heard, heads nod in agreement when it is suggested that 'Merchant Navys' brought electrifying speed to Wessex before the third-rail arrived or diesels chattered.

The 'Duchesses' were indeed superb and the Bulleid Pacifics did bring splendour to the last decade of steam on the Southern, but the position was different on the LNER. Here the Pacific idea and a big engine policy would, as it were, create the whole shape and concept of the railway. Two main reasons for this phenomena, one the long period, evolutionary perhaps, over which the Pacific type developed on that railway, the second contained in a name — Gresley, who would make the Pacific period an epoch. The seeds were already germinating before the formation of the LNER, the rising arch of inspiration finding its highest point with the coming of the A4s, though the falling curve of postwar Pacifics was not without its own glory.

A brief look at passenger locomotive trends on the big four in the early years of the Grouping clearly shows either a firm grip of future locomotive policies, or an uncertainty which, for a number of reasons, made for late development at least in terms of steam motive power.

On the Great Western, the seal of Churchward was firmly imprinted. Here was the supreme example of a really great locomotive designer evolving a formula of locomotive building long to survive him and, in its basic form, would remain throughout the company's life. Though he built one lonely Pacific, the 4-6-0 became the chassis into which he poured all the ideas and theory of a superb steam engineer, the soundness of these was such that they dominated steam locomotive practice for the rest of its natural life on the Great Western and elsewhere.

The Southern became very quickly involved with massive suburban electrification schemes, the new traction being earmarked initially for the intensive system of lines in the counties, south of London forming the heart and body of the new railway. Steam locomotive building to supply traction for the spidery extended tentacles of the remainder would be inclined to take second place. New steam designs were modest in scope, indeed nearly 20 years elapsed before anything as large as a Pacific emerged on the Southern.

The LMS made a faltering start with a, not unexpected, bias, at least initially, towards Midland small engine policy. It required a decade to pass and the coming of a future giant of the locomotive world, William Stanier, before the locomotive policy acquired real direction. This quickly showed influences attributable to Swindon and a leaning towards the 4-6-0. I say this knowing full well that ultimately 50 magnificent Pacifics were built, but remembering that an overwhelmingly large proportion of LMS passenger traffic was moved by 'Scots', 'Patriots', 'Jubilees', Class 5s, which between them mustered well over 1,000 locomotives.

The LNER differed from the other three railways in many respects two in particular being a contributory factor in moulding the basic character of the line. These, one topographical the other human, were to become inextricably linked with every aspect of LNER policy and identity.

From the beginning the new railway became dominated by the great main line forming its backbone, which, commencing modestly enough at the Kings Cross buffer stops, eventually penetrated deep into the Scottish northland. As a railway racing route and one seeing the daily passage of the most famous named train in the world, this most romantic railway would become the mainspring of the LNER and remain involved in the aspirations and achievement of the new company during the whole of the near quarter century it existed. One searches for words to describe the special atmosphere of the East Coast line, the glamour, the almost heroic parade of great locomotives. Great Northern, North Eastern, North British Atlantics powering long trains in relay. The pageantry of the Gresley era, when green then blue Pacifics stretched themselves in lithe splendour from end to end of this celebrated railway, being the high water mark, though the 'Deltics' renewed the old dash and style for a time.

Fate also bestowed blessings on the new railway in the choice of the Chief Mechanical Engineer, who proved to be a fine engineer and one of brilliant imaginative mind who would impress his own very potent form of glamour. I use the word fate, but is it not true that an unseen hand sometimes seems to guide. Boardroom decision or Prime Minister's choice, the element of chance is always there, rightly so from the cogitation of mere mortals. Doubtless the history of the LNER would have been quite different, had now forgotten men not chosen Gresley. It is said the moment will find the man, the LNER was fortunate, they found theirs in a designer who transcended technical expertise to a degree that brought him to a high plane of both engineering and artistic achievement. His energy and drive were responsible for the 1930s becoming the era of streamlined trains, high speed, illustrious locomotives. The charm of the man leapt from the surface of the most ordinary black and white photograph. A whole generation were fascinated by

the personality and the machines of his creation. The LNER of prewar days captured the imagination of the general public and engineering world alike, most credit for which goes to the CME. A visionary well aware of the need to introduce a heightened sense of appeal and adventure in railway travel, a factor that seems to have been rediscovered in the 1970s.

As a schoolboy I spent many hours' observation by the lineside of the loop from Fairfield Junction to Manchester Central, the passing of each apple green engine, especially if a 'Sandringham', setting off my imagination. With the miracle that it is the mind's eye switched on I could see distant eastern lands of fen and dyke with rolling windswept pasture focusing the vision on far away great houses. A promised land to which the green engines would hurry back after a brief visit to this darker place of soot terraced brick and industry. Of course Pacifics never appeared on the line but long before I was out of short pants the letters LNER came to represent things magical in the locomotive world. The seed was sown, Doncaster became Mecca to which the head always turned, dreams finally coming to fruition in mid-1937 when a long-awaited pilgrimage became possible. A whole day to be spent on the platforms of the most celebrated station on the East Coast main line. A few hours to become suspended moments in a lifetime which constantly the memory leaps the years to recapture. Like all life's greatest experiences they can never be repeated no matter how many times you return.

In a few hours I saw all the locomotives I had dreamed about. The first Pacific No 2747 *Coranach* chose to arrive light engine off the shed. Mentally I did a dance of joy, is it real or a dream? Would I awake to find an opened *Wonder Book of Railways* and the shadow rather than the substance? Swiftly I became aware of reality, the senses invaded overwhelmed by sight and sound as more pictures from the railway books came springing solidly to life. I yearned for time to slip into slow motion as the grandstand, of which I was a solitary occupant, provided views in profusion of the passing parade. Green, silver, blue Pacifics racing through, rousing the passions, causing blood to flow quicker, in my own veins of course for I saw no other spectator moved to cheer. The up and down 'Silver Jubilees' hurtled through like something pre-dating the space age, the grey metallic appearance somewhat cold and clinical compared to the external opulence of the

'Coronation' and 'West Riding Limited' in their garter blue. These elite trains, almost brand new, inclined to overshadow everything else, with splendour of colour, fine names and impressive streamlined locomotives. With streamlining being the vogue of the 1930s the A4s were almost household words gracing the pages of newspaper and magazine. They certainly had glamour, each one being a thrilling sight in its own right, but for the space of those few hours the A3s remained the apple of my eye, my attention being continually riveted to these sleek green charmers providing motive power for many other substantial important expresses. Those other 'sleek green charmers' the new 'Green Arrows' were also much in evidence, fast gaining a reputation for speed and performance that had them spoken in the same breath as the Pacifics. The tally, impressive though it is, takes no account of the second division. Great Northern Atlantics, old in age but still good enough to run some of the important Pullman trains. 'Sandringhams', 'Hunts', and a variety of pre-Grouping Atlantics and 4-4-0s etc made a seemingly endless list on that long golden day. Never before or since have I seen such a galaxy of colour or variety of great locomotives, a spell was cast which fortunately I have never recovered from!

Ironically I never again saw the LNER main line at the height of its glory, declaration of war on 3 September 1939 saw the grand schemes intended to inject our railways with new life snuffed out like a light. It's an ill wind however, for out of national misfortune came one tiny fragment of personal good fortune, by mid-1941 I had donned a blue uniform and, thanks to HM Government, found the key which opened the door to extensive rail travel and a multitude of locoshed visits. Pacifics, both East and West Coast, became very familiar, but despite a host of new and exciting experiences nothing quite transcended that wonderful day in mid-1937.

In mid-1941 Nigel Gresley died, widely mourned by enthusiast and railwayman alike. No matter that he was near to statutory retirement, for the man seemed an immortal. The normal human wasting processes, the gradual diminishing of creative and physical powers common to most people, did not seem to enter our thoughts where Gresley was concerned. One thing was certain, life for any successor would not be easy, bridging the stride of a giant never is. Unfortunately the seat of power at Doncaster seemed about to be occupied by a man

representing a different school of thought and ideas. Edward Thompson seemed, at least to admirers of Gresley, to herald a twilight period, a new dark age of austerity in the locomotive world. Especially when the rebuilding of older engines hinted at loss of symmetry and proportion. Intended to give greater economy of working the refurbishing of some older classes would be the cause of deep distress and misunderstanding in the world of railways.

New designs eventually included Pacifics of a somewhat ungainly aspect, and a superb 4-6-0. Destined to become his most brilliant success, the B1s, as the class became designated by the LNER, were the little giants so badly needed to replace the now creaking giants of another age. Great Atlantics, imposing pre-Grouping 4-6-0s, quickly succumbed to the nimble 'Springboks'. The Thompson Pacifics were never especially distinguished in performance despite the thermal and mechanical advances which may have been expected in the decade since the last Gresley Pacific arrived on the scene. They did however maintain the LNER big engine policy which in turn would be continued by Thompson's successor, Peppercorn.

Of the Thompson rebuilds, an early conversion, or travesty according to your point of view, were all six of Gresley's mighty P2 2-8-2s. Whether innocent or, as some thought, an intentional desecration of his predecessor's work will never really be known. Though it is unlikely that a more tactless or emotive beginning could have been made.

It was my good fortune, during a brief period in the early war years, to see all the P2s at work in their original eight coupled condition, therefore the shock of seeing a rebuild for the first time was all the more acute. It happened while serving with the RAF in south-west Scotland during 1943/44. Many times during this period I enjoyed the privilege of visiting Eastfield and other locomotive depots in the Glasgow area, in the process becoming friendly with several shed foremen and one in particular at Eastfield. He was a North British man with a very possessive feeling for the Mikados since he considered them almost a Scottish class. He accepted any unresolved faults in the engines as a small price to pay in return for them being worked entirely within the old North British section. Such was the sense of pride engendered by the old companies — how sadly lacking today. On one or two occasions we discussed the rumoured rebuild of a P2 at

Doncaster, both hoping it would not become fact. However on my visit of 18 March 1944 he greeted me with sad face and invited me along to Cowlairs Works' yard. The clean gleaming machine standing there carried a familiar name *Thane of Fife*, and number 2005, but the shape was wrong and a pair of driving wheels were missing. We viewed, with mutual dismay, this black phoenix risen from the ashes of the 2-8-2 and wondered what Gresley would have made of it. Perhaps our feelings of distaste would have been less acute had the name and number differed from the original. My immediate reaction, albeit an emotional one, was to see it as a symbol — the doll like image of an adversary pierced by a 1,000 pins, though in the light of shocks to follow I had little cause to see it otherwise.

Argument about these huge machines, the biggest and most powerful passenger locomotive to run on a British railway, will long continue. Some saw them as the ultimate white elephant, others as the answer to the problems of high speed haulage of heavy passenger trains and the rapid movement of freight. Sadly the seeds of greatness they may have carried within never had time to germinate let alone flower. So many imponderables surround the short life of the P2s. Would postwar refinement have produced the nucleus of a greatly improved heavy passenger unit for the last 20 years of steam? Or were they, like Brunels broad gauge (if the comparison doesn't seem too incongruous) a brilliant concept that just did not fit the particular time/environment sequence? One thing is certain, they rank among the great tragi/heroic figures of railway history. Heroic for the courageous enterprise behind the boldness of the concept. Heroic too in the nobility of their bearing, yet tragic for being doomed to stalk a darkened stage.

Ironically hindsight shows that Gresley, in producing the V2s and A4s, had already solved the problems mentioned in the second sentence of the previous paragraph. Perhaps, overawed by sheer size and majesty of the 2-8-2s and the fact Gresley designed them, reaction to the rebuilding was almost inevitably emotional rather than practical.

It may have been pure coincidence that the first Gresley Pacific to suffer the 'treatment' was none other than No 4470 *Great Northern*, though it is hard to believe this historic engine just happened to be around for shopping when rebuilding plans were ready to be put into operation. Ulterior motive? Well even given the benefit of the doubt it still remains an action remarkably lacking in tact. When the engine emerged from Doncaster Works in 1945 many enthusiasts viewed the result with consternation. Vanished were the classic lines and symmetrical appearance, what remained seemed, at least visually, to be an assembly of dissimilar bits and pieces from around the workshop, including a front bogie that appeared about to run away from the engine. The care and attention to visual detail which made the new B1 one of the most attractive 4-6-0s ever to run on rails, was strangely lacking in the rebuilt Pacific. All Thompson's Pacifics suffered from this ugly duckling look, as if he could never quite make up his mind on what made a well balanced relationship between cylinders, bogies, running plate etc. It remained for Peppercorn to slot things into place when his A1/A2 Pacifics brought a return to beauty of outline.

Gresley admirers were relieved when plans to treat other members of the A3 class (which would probably have included the *Flying Scotsman*) to the grotesquery suffered by No 4470 were shelved. Ironically the A3s, still around 15-20 years after the No 4470 happening, continued to produce performance levels that would keep them in the front rank of British Pacifics. Throughout their lives they remained virtually unchanged in appearance except for the double chimney and smoke deflectors carried in the last few years. There may have been internal refinements to give rejuvenation in old age, which would serve to prove how unnecessary was the untimely, ugly rebuild of ill fame.

Argument always returns. A question mark hangs like the Democlesian sword, ready to fall and demolish glib solutions. The question — did Thompson have ulterior motive for what, in his name, was done to some of the Gresley engines? Do we see genuine desire to improve the work of a predecessor, or the results of frustration at having remained in the shadows for so long? Of course we will never know the absolute truth, but we can search around for a few clues to cast some light into the darkness of the mystery. Study, for example the apparent difference of character of the two men. Here, in the abrasive rubbing of personality, is perhaps a key to unlock one segment of an intriguing puzzle, and I believe the photographic portrait will help any investigation.

A study of photographs of the two engineers does

I think reveal something of their character, every nuance of expression suggesting men of widely different personality and temperament. The genial ebullient spirit of Gresley almost leaps off the paper, and there is more than a trace of flamboyance. Note how the eyes twinkle, but isn't there more than a hint of arrogance in their gaze? The whole appearance is aristocratic, yet a larger than life personality beams through. You can imagine the archetype, wise and benevolent uncle, who would dominate the family gathering, full of anecdotes, loved by the youngsters. Confidence beams through in every line of expression — confidence, the word tells everything, of a man at ease sure of his own powers and clear in the direction of his life's work. The very positive attributes of character probably helped give the man a superb mastery of the problems he set himself to solve. Man of genius? Emotive words, I use them knowing full well some eyebrows of doubt may be raised, yet I am sure Gresley had creative inventive powers to such an extraordinary degree as to justify there use. If the assumption is correct then one can go on to say that genius is never easy to live or work with, especially if the face does not quite fit. There are implications that Thompson's face did not always fit with Gresley, possibly for reasons beyond the understanding of even the men themselves.

Thompson looked spare of frame and a rather sensitive aquiline face peering from photographs has more than a trace of wistful wariness. I imagine he was shy and retiring by nature, though doubtless necessity forced him to come part way out of his shell. He is reputed to have been strict with staff and a stickler for correctness of dress, and by all accounts his appointment with power at Doncaster brought changes savouring somewhat of sweeping bits of the pro Gresley faction under the carpet. Contradictions, yet would it be unusual for an easy nature, probably being disciplined by a very determined mind, to react unexpectedly.

Indications are that Thompson was a quiet man, perhaps in a way quite vulnerable, maybe easily hurt by the cutting remark which he may not have found easy to forgive or forget. Gresley was probably quite scathing at times in his attitude towards his staff, though his may have been less intentional than part of the manner of the man. Feathers may have been ruffled at times, but would a man of Thompson's calibre have consciously wished to return a hurt? I

somehow doubt it, well certainly not to the extent of rebuilding a predecessors work in order to tarnish his reputation. But — and this is the sixty-four dollar question — who knows to what degree the conscious mind is influenced and affected by the unfathomable subconscious?

Thompson's retirement in June 1946 brought a return to more aesthetically acceptable shapes in the new Pacifics designed by his successor A. H. Peppercorn, a known Gresley disciple. The new Pacifics, Class AI/A2, produced in the very short time before nationalisation, had a sleekness and beauty of line placing them second only to Gresley's evergreen A3s. They were to keep company with the A3s for the rest of their lives and, of equal importance, provide a level of performance equal to anything being produced elsewhere in the country. They were a living proof that even in the most advanced steam locomotive design parts could be assembled into a most distinctive classic shape. Indeed it is interesting to speculate what might have happened had the fates decreed for Peppercorn to take the reigns of office in 1941!

Though the postwar Pacifics did splendid work in the 1950s they never superseded the A3/A4s. They were fine engines that had the misfortune to follow in the wheel treads of what, in the case of the A4s, was a near perfect combination of mechanical and thermal dimensions. Indeed the A4s were a consumation of the locomotive builders' art, the sort of perfection that just eluded so many and allowed Gresley to move into the realms of greatness in this his most outstanding achievement in locomotive design.

The Peppercorn Pacifics, along with the A4s and the amazingly rejuvenated A3s, provided adequate power for the East Coast main line for the remaining period of steam. For over 30 years in successive generations the 4-6-2 dominated the thinking, style and prestige of the LNER. A phenomena that had to happen once in history. Never before, or since, has one man and one type of locomotive so clearly represented the image of a railway.

*Above right:* **Haymarket shed on 21 May 1957. Class A3 No 60041** *Salmon Trout.* **The author, in typical adult gricer uniform of the day, stands by the front buffer beam.** *Alan Blencowe*

*Right:* **Huntingdon on 20 May 1957, Class A3 60108** *Gay Crusader* **on the 8.35am semi-fast to Kings Cross.** *Alan Blencowe*

*Left:* Doncaster Works on 10 May 1959, Class A3 No 60108 *Gay Crusader* (Class A1 No 60158 *Aberdonian* in rear). This particular shopping would have seen No 60108 fitted with the double chimney. *Raymond Keeley*

*Centre left:* Down express near Hitchin on 12 August 1961. Class A3 No 60065 *Knight of Thistle.* A rather murky day and the trail of steam seems to emphasise the speed of the train. The engine, around 37 years of age at the time of the photograph, appears little changed over the years with the exception of the double chimney. A few weeks later however the appearance would dramatically alter with the fitting of the rather ugly smoke deflectors carried by some members of the class in the last few years of their life. *Alan Blencowe*

*Below left:* New England (Peterborough) shed on 20 July 1963. Class A3 No 60044 *Melton.* The photograph shows clearly how radically the thoroughbred look of the A3s was changed by the rather unsightly deflectors. The racehorse well and truly blinkered. *Alan Blencowe*

*Above right:* Doncaster shed on 23 May 1958. Class A3 No 60107 *Royal Lancer.* After 35 years of life the old engine still looks every inch the Gresley masterpiece. In the author's opinion the most elegant Pacific type ever to run on rails. *Alan Blencowe*

*Below right:* Doncaster Works on 10 May 1959. Class A3 No 60088 *Book Law.* The engine awaits shopping and will eventually emerge from the plant restored for a new lease of life and with new head gear in the form of a double chimney. *Raymond Keeley*

*Left:* Class A4 No 60003 *Andrew K. McCosh* on down fish empties, approaching Everton signalbox, c1960. *Alan Blencowe*

*Centre left:* New England (Peterborough) shed. Class A4 No 60017 *Silver Fox*. At the time of the photograph, 20 July 1963, the old engine, then nearly 28 years of age had been removed from main line duties and was within a few months of withdrawal. The lines of a racer are still there and the clear shape of the fox reminds of the silvered glory that was. *Alan Blencowe*

*Bottom:* Huntingdon on 23 July 1962. Class A4 No 60017 *Silver Fox*, on down stopping train. Just 12 months earlier than the previous picture, with the engine now looking rather less than her years and in decidely better shape, at least externally. *Alan Blencowe*

*Above right:* Sandy on 4 August 1962. Class A4 No 60025 *Falcon* hauling a down van train. The line in the background is the LNWR Cambridge to Bedford line, curving west to cross the Great Northern main line a few hundred yards north of the spot in the photograph. *Alan Blencowe*

*Below right:* Newcastle Central on 21 May 1958. Class A4 No 60018 *Sparrow Hawk* on the northbound 'North Briton'. The A4 had just taken over from A3 No 60086 *Gainsborough* which had brought the train from Leeds. *Raymond Keeley*

*Above left:* Retford on 5 July 1958.
Class A4 No 60025 *Falcon* on a down
express. The wall on the left was a
favourite perch for locospotters of the
day, how many I wonder still retain
the interest 20 years later?
*Raymond Keeley*

*Left:* Dundee-Edinburgh train leaving
North Queensferry on 29 May 1963.
Class A4 No 60012 *Commonwealth of
Australia*.  *Alan Blencowe*

*Top:* Doncaster on 23 May 1958.
Class A1 No 60158 *Aberdonian* on the
up 'White Rose'.  *Raymond Keeley*

*Above:* Darlington 22 May 1958:
Class A1 No 60132 *Marmion* on up
express.  *Raymond Keeley*

*Right:* Leeds City before rebuilding,
photo taken on 31 August 1957. Class
A2 No 60539 *Bronzino* facing west on
a Newcastle, via Harrogate, train.
*Raymond Keeley*

# 'Green Arrows' and Moguls

The 'Green Arrows' appeared when Gresley was at the height of his powers, during those hectic, memorable, earth shaking (at least from the railway enthusiasts point of view) years of the middle and late 1930s. Designed as a very powerful mixed traffic locomotive, able in general service, to range over the greater part of the main line system, they succeeded brilliantly. History would eventually see them as probably the best large mixed traffic engine ever built in Britain. An honoured position that events only just in the future would quickly help them to qualify for.

It is unlikely the V2s, as they were designated by the LNER, were intended to work on equal terms with the Pacifics, but they soon showed themselves capable of performing any of the jobs normally the perogative of the 4-6-2s, which included occasionally deputising for A4s on the streamlined trains. Both in haulage capacity and speed is soon became clear they were second to none, with the exception of the A4s. The outbreak of war soon gave the V2s opportunity to show their great power and versatility, the 20-coach trains worked regularly up and down the Great Northern main line powered by the Pacifics and 'Green Arrows' without discrimination, proved the wisdom of Gresley's big engine policy. My good fortune, during a few months in mid-1942 was to be stationed at a large airfield near Peterborough, spending many off duty hours roaming the platforms of the North station. Twenty coaches were the norm, occasionally there were more, the most I actually saw on one train was 26!

I recall one memorable journey when returning to Stamford on an LMS all stations local. The ex-Midland branch parallels the LNER main line for the first six and a half miles out of Peterborough then veers off to the west. Distances between stations varied, in some cases being sufficient to allow the class 2P 4-4-0 to gather a little speed, especially as there were not usually more than about three bogies behind the tender. The train had left Walton with the 2P cantering leisurely into its stride emitting the usual gruff, ha-huff — ha-huff, from the chimney top. The tender and first carriage wriggling slightly with the effort.

Being the only occupant of the compartment I spread out a little perusing the nice haul of numbers gleaned from the New England area, meanwhile keeping an alert eye on the Great Northern main line. As the 2P slowed for the Helpston stop I caught sight of a distant cloud of smoke well down the main line. After the brief pause the 4-4-0 quickly, but with effort, struggled back to around 40mph, but the distant flurry of smoke was rapidly catching up. To the railway enthusiast, there can be no greater excitement, no greater lift to the spirit than the sight of a thoroughbred steam locomotive (or diesel locomotive for that matter) taking a grip on a sizeable train. Once again I experienced the nerve tingling sensation generated by such a timeless moment.

The train, swiftly pacing up behind the Leicester Local, was of great length. But judging by the determined look of the engine (all the Gresley non streamlined Pacifics and the V2s had this determined confident look) such a small item as half a dozen or so extra carriages would act more as a challenge than a deterrent. The engine, a V2, now almost alongside, had all the appearance of a runner, head down, arms and legs bent in a movement pulling the body forward. The upward lift of running plate over driving wheels and the drop under the firebox appearing as skirts lifted the less to impede the pace. The backward stream of smoke and steam demonstrating the urgency of movement, well reflected in the fireman's steady motion with the shovel.

The 2P smelling chase in the air, strained every sinew, whipping the little train up toward the 50mph mark. One almost felt there was a racing pulse down amongst that jangling inside valve gear, to no avail however for I reckon the express was well into the 50s. The carriages, in apparently endless procession, rat atat tatted past, packed to the corridors, 18, 19, 20, 21, — I never ceased to marvel. Suddenly the show was over as the trains veered away from each other, green fields separating the quietly galumphing 4-4-0 from the long, northbound, clattering caravan the now distant V2 roaring defiance at the gradient, a leonine mane of smoke and steam evidence of great moving limbs of steel. The 2-6-2, young, sleek, powerfully boned, sound in wind and limb, always ready to give an olympian display of energy and pyrotechnics. The perfect extrovert, bringing this mere mortal to an overawed silence. The old 4-4-0, tired of limb and just a little chesty, finding even a handful of carriages a burden, gratefully looked forward to each station pause, relieved that the stirring of competitive spirit had been of such short duration.

The sinuous exit, north or southbound, from Peterborough was not of the easiest, and, like the northern start out of York, seemed to find the weakness of the big Gresley engines, their inclination to slip. Getting these huge trains of heavy bogie stock on the move was no joke, especially as several of the carriages could be curving out of the south end of the station. I know it was wartime and 20-coach plus trains were part of our grim resolve to see the thing through but, to the solitary spectator at the top end of that platform the northern start was pure exhilarating entertainment. A shuddering roar cum slip followed even the the gentlest opening of a regulator, then came something like the sound of a well oiled sewing machine, in the A4s it was more like a soft shoe shuffle. At least it showed power was there, steam passages almost unbelievably free and flowing.

Finally all this unleashed fury came to grips where it mattered — on terra firma! Very slowly carriages crowded with khaki and blue began to glide by, the bogies passing over rail joints in seeming endless clatter. Away in the distance a column of smoke and steam showed Pacific or Prairie girding its loins in preparation for the long haul up to Stoke Tunnel.

From the appearance of No 4771 in mid-1936 until the demise of the class some 30 years later, they enjoyed great popularity with both layman and enginemen. An example of the esteem in which they were held lies behind the comment frequently heard in the 1940s and 1950s. The engines that won the war. A nostalgic exaggeration of course, but on the other hand if Britain had remained at peace in the 1940s the V2s may have helped win a quite different sort of battle for the LNER. There is no doubt the concept of this class leaned more to the provision of a locomotive capable of revolutionising the rapid movement of certain classes of freight, than of creating a new rival for the Pacifics. They were just beginning to show their potential when World War II commenced. The engines that first showed the possibilities in this field were the K3 Moguls, their pioneering could be seen to have fathered the idea which culminated in the swift moving liner trains of today.

The Gresley Moguls in the early years after World War I, had shown the possibility of a small wheeled mixed traffic locomotive with a well designed front end, hauling prodigious loads at speeds up to the mile a minute range. (Perhaps the whole idea of motorways for heavy traffic should have been called into question 40-50 years ago?) The K3s had a large and efficient boiler (the largest diameter ever placed on a locomotive of such modest size, in this country). Ample capacity to boil water, a good front end, and very good adhesion meant that the high tractive effort was more than just a figure on a table of dimensions. They made a sensational debut in the early 1920s and doubtless helped to pave the way for Gresleys future large engine policy. In those early years on the Great Northern main line they produced evidence of power output and performance well beyond anything any other Mogul in this country would have been expected to attain. They were at least the equal of any mixed traffic 4-6-0 produced in Britain, their exceptional versatility being proved quite early in their careers by the ease with which fast goods or heavy passenger trains were worked, especially during some of the troubled industrial periods of the early 1920s.

In my experience any type of train was fair game for the K3s in the Manchester area, I saw them work every sort, two coach locals on the Guide Bridge —

Manchester Central service, the Liverpool-Hull trains, heavy goods over Woodhead, excursions, it was all the same to these grand engines.

Excursions! how I remember them before the war, standing on packed platforms at Hyde Road or Levenshulme stations with sandwiches and bottle of water, hoping for one of those rare glimpses of the sea that occasionally came the way of the working class city child. The venue being invariably Southport. They ran via the south Manchester loop to Throstle Nest Junction, thence Cheshire lines to Southport Lord Street. If you had a K3 on, which was quite often, you fully expected to get there and back on time — and a schoolboy with limited railway knowledge had that sort of confidence. Sometimes it would be a J39 0-6-0 or one of the older Great Central 4-4-0s, then you didn't feel quite so sure!

On one occasion, in the Aintree area where the Cheshire lines and the LMS (L&Y) Liverpool-Preston ran parallel for a distance, our K3 with 10 on met an ex-Midland type 0-6-0 with six on. A situation with slightly comic overtones then developed. Here was a rather sleek swashbuckling 2-6-0 thick boiler seemingly packed with power, taking every opportunity to show the full potential of mixed traffic driving wheels for high speed running. Smooth syncopation from three cylinders, a sound suggesting agility, leaping limbs, throwing out a challenge, the flinging down of a gauntlet — but would it be taken up? One could imagine the smirk appearing on the smokebox door of the K3 as it glanced sideways at the plodding rival now shaking with the jerky angular see-saw motion so emphasised when they attempted anything over 30mph. One sensed the weariness of the elderly engine pressed by this smooth competitor toward speed unfitting, ungainly and undignified for a small wheeled 0-6-0.

Seizing the gauntlet, the old engine had a go, smoke and steam poured gruffly from the chimney as an attempt was made to hurry up the sedately moving inside motion, connecting rods lunged angrily causing the long, disembodied looking, coupling rod to swing frenziedly up and down, as if hell bent on tearing its wheels of the axles. Gradually the flashy charmer began to overhaul the cloth capped workhorse, now fussing along in the chesty way of the 4Fs when attempting a little speed. It hadn't a chance, we passed it easily within the mile

and a half before the two lines veered apart. The occasional railway race added zest to any journey since they were usually unexpected and always seemed to bring out the spontaneous competitive spirit latent in many steam locomotive drivers in those days.

The K3s were useful, versatile engines, possibly the only Gresley six coupled type you could imagine starting a 16-coach train north from York without the driver worrying over much about wearing the rail down to the chairs! But they were part of a supporting cast of thousands, living out a life of comparative obscurity, while the super stars of the rail strutted the pages of practice and performance flamboyant, glittering in the bosom of public esteem. The 'Green Arrows' always remained among those super stars, born in the last half of the decade of the 1930s during the final flowering of Nigel Gresley's genius. When he died at the early age of 65 in 1941 we can at least be fairly certain he had reached the zenith in his life's work, and the V2s were certainly part of that peak of achievement.

The one real enigma of that peak is the P2 2-8-2, it remains so because the turn of events precluded any chance of proving conclusively the advantages, or otherwise, of eight coupled wheels for fast, heavy passenger work in Britain. I believe many enthusiasts of my middle aged generation feel more strongly about Thompson's conversion of the 2-8-2s, than the isolated carve up of No 4470. At least the rest of A3s remained to go on to even greater glory. With the P2s there is a definite frustration, here we thought was the germ of a great idea whose development became stifled by war, then completely stamped out.

I have used the word enigma quite deliberately in connection with the P2s, for it is almost the perfect riddle. We incline to make Thompson the scapegoat for denying us the excitement of seeing a 2-8-2 at work on the postwar East Coast main line. But, and I say this as a decided Gresley enthusiast, I do have an impression that Gresley himself turned away from these engines even before the outbreak of war.

The original concept of the 2-8-2 was to provide higher power on the Edinburgh-Aberdeen route, though the choice of eight coupled wheels seems strange for a line with such an abundance of snake like curvature. The continued concentration of all six engines in Scotland does, to my view, hint at relegation, almost as if Gresley himself hadn't decided what to do about them. By September 1939, with the country at war, any decisions he may have been considering are likely to have been placed to one side.

Postwar operation gave the V2s further opportunity to prove their almost universal competence in dealing with all types of traffic over the most diverse routes. Thus they came into their own on the Edinburgh-Aberdeen and the Waverley line. Maybe Thompson's decision to rebuild was no more than we may have expected from Gresley. Perhaps, he would have discarded the P2s in favour of what, in the 'Green Arrows', became Britain's best high power mixed traffic locomotive and, one of his most outstanding designs.

*Below:* **Down goods passing Sandy on 4 August 1962. Class V2 No 60868. The LNWR Cambridge-Bedford line can be clearly seen in the background.** *Alan Blencowe*

*Above:* Class V2 No 60884 on an up express approaching Doncaster on 23 May 1958. The vintage LNER 2nd and 3rd coaches will be noted. *Raymond Keeley*

*Below:* Darlington Shed, 21 May 1958: Class V2 No 60836 and Class A8 No 69881. The mountain of coal in the foreground is evidence of the many awkward vantage points used by the photographer in steam days. It was usually a case of scramble, slither — click, and hope for the best, in this case a very low evening sun gives the impression that the two engines are about to be engulfed by the aforementioned mountain! *Raymond Keeley*

*Above:* Kings Cross c1949. A begrimed V2 No 60859 backing away, probably to top shed. *Anthony Keeley*

*Below:* Up goods approaching Doncaster on 10 June 1959. Class V2 No 60858. *Raymond Keeley*

*Above:* Down local passenger train approaching Huntingdon on 27 April 1957 behind Class V2 No 60832. Note the parcels van behind the engine, which appears to be of GNR vintage. *Alan Blencowe*

*Below:* Doncaster shed on 10 May 1959. Class K3 No 61804. The photograph clearly shows the sturdy but stumpy lines of these powerful locomotives. *Raymond Keeley*

*Above:* Passenger train leaving Bletchley on the Oxford
line on 4 March 1961. Class K3 No 61880.   *Alan Blencowe*

*Below:* Manchester Central on 19 March 1958. At
8.20am Class K3 No 61832, running late with the 7.32am
all stations local from Guide Bridge via Fallowfield.
*Raymond Keeley*

*Above:* Class K3 No 61910 running light through Reddish North station on 13 September 1958. The shed code being 9G which is Northwich suggests that the engine is bound for Gorton, possibly for routine maintenance. *Raymond Keeley*

*Below:* The turntable at Bletchley on 6 May 1961. Class K3 No 61801 of Cambridge shed (31A) had worked a local passenger train on this very useful cross-country branch, a service alas no longer available. *Alan Blencowe*

*Above:* York station south end on 5 July 1961. Class K3 No 61942 on the up main through line with a train of bolster and flat wagons. *Raymond Keeley*

*Below:* Sheffield Victoria on 19 August 1959. Class K3 No 61882 on the 5.50pm Leicester. *Raymond Keeley*

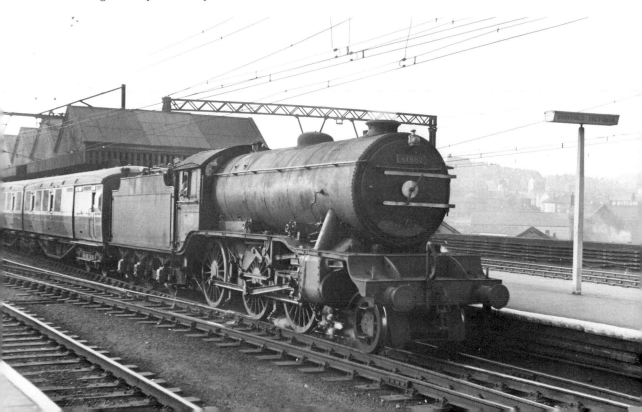

*Left:* **Woodwalton (approx six miles north of Huntingdon) on 4 April 1957 Class K3 No 61979 on up ballast train.** *Alan Blencowe*

*Below left:* **Bletchley shed on 6 October 1959. Class K3 No 61937 of 31A (Cambridge) being turned after bringing in a local from Cambridge.** *Alan Blencowe*

*Above:* **Eastfield shed on 23 May 1957, Class K2 No 61787 *Loch Quoich* awaits attention to her centre drivers. The K2s, one of Gresley's earliest designs for the Great Northern Railway, had long lives. After the Grouping some were transferred to Scotland for working the West Highland line. They were an undoubted success and were probably the reason for him producing the K4s especially for working on the West Highland. The K4s were possibly the most compact package of tractive power placed on LNER rails, being, on a theoretical tractive effort basis, more powerful than most of the large passenger locomotives running in Britain.** *Raymond Keeley*

*Right:* **Cowlairs Works on 23 May 1957. Class K2 No 61726 awaits shopping. Note the shed plate (38A) also the home depot name, Colwick spelt out on the buffer beam. It was not unusual for Cowlairs to service certain classes of engines from English depots. I remember during the war seeing Class J39 0-6-0s from far afield awaiting attention outside the works, or at Eastfield depot nearby, newly emerged with a gloss sheen that would all too quickly be lost.** *Raymond Keeley*

# The 'Sandringhams' and B1s

## with thoughts on pre-Grouping 4-6-0s

During the last 50 years of steam in Britain the 4-6-0, if only because of the numbers built, was assured of its place as the most popular type for a wide range of passenger work. But despite this it never dominated locomotive practice on the LNER as it did on the GWR and to a slightly lesser extent the LMS. On the GWR under Churchward, the type steadily developed to become standard for most passenger and mixed traffic work for the rest of the company's life. The LMS was not quite so single minded, due in early post-Grouping days to Midland small engine policy. However, with the arrival of Stanier the 4-6-0 began to play an important role, reaching, in the Class 5 and rebuilt 'Scots', a standard of perfection never surpassed anywhere.

The situation on the LNER was quite different and for good reason. In the first place the old companies which formed the LNER were, with the exception of the Great Eastern, lines dominated by the success of 4-4-0s and Atlantics. Even on the Great Eastern the 1500 class 4-6-0s never overshadowed the legendary 'Claud Hamilton' 4-4-0s. A second, perhaps infinitely greater reason for brushing aside any arguments favouring the 4-6-0, came in the form of one man, striding like a colossus across the railway scene of the 1920s and 1930s — Gresley.

I believe Brunel and Gresley were the greatest of the more unconventional railway engineers. Both were flamboyant and extrovert by nature, though this in itself is of no great significance, but add inventiveness and originality of mind and the ingredients for thinking and creating in a grand manner are present. These attributes place them in a class apart from many railway engineers who, in the main, were content to develop and build on existing practice. Brunel and Gresley were the great innovators, when others tried the result was usually failure. Bulleid was perhaps the most outstanding recent example of the inventive ingenious mind whose revolutionary ideas were largely defeated in practice.

Gresley, man of the grand vision, intended to bring a big engine policy to fruition on the LNER. The first shaping of the theme could already be seen in No 4470, sire of one of the most famous and successful locomotive types ever to be built. Clearly the 4-6-0 did not play a very dominant part in the grand designs that lay ahead. However in 1928 the 'Sandringham' class 4-6-0 emerged, they were to prove as good as other similar sized engines of their time, but would be the only 4-6-0 built by Gresley. It seemed as if he had glanced briefly aside from the main direction of his thinking, which I imagine, would be with ideas finally to emerge as the noble designs of the mid-1930s. This long term planning plus a need for economy were probably two of the reasons for perpetuating certain pre-Grouping passenger types. To this end fortune favoured him, through his inheriting from the pre-Grouping companies a first class locomotive stock in the medium power range. The Great Northern, North Eastern and North British Atlantics, plus some of the best 4-4-0s then running, held easy sway on all the main lines. The retention of these, and in some cases adding to their numbers or rebuilding, indicated that there was no urgent need for new medium passenger power during this period. The two notable designs, in this category that were built, namely the D49 4-4-0s and the 'Sandringhams', could be considered more in terms of augmenting than replacing existing classes.

I have suggested the 'Sandringhams' were no more than one of the sparks thrown off the Gresley anvil as he forged away towards his chef d'oeuvre, the A4, thus perhaps implying that the B17 was inferior. This indeed was far from the case, since they always performed with great distinction, particularly on the Great Eastern and Great Central sections, where competition from some of the cream of the pre-Grouping classes was intense. But it had to be admitted that like their excellent contemporaries, the D49, they suffered from waiting in the wings while the stage was taken by Pacifics, Prairies and Mikados acting out all the exciting events which occupied the Great Northern main line during the decade of the 1930s.

One happening that caused the 'Sandringhams' to occupy a very special place in my early boyhood, was the evening vigil on Ardwick station to see the passing of the 9 o'clock. The waiting time was usually spent in the company of another lad with a predilection for all things LNER. The venue, a couple of miles from my home, entailed a cycle ride along the busy Hyde Road, usually in the company of a variety of other wheeled vehicles. These included horse drawn railway vans and wagons which lurched and clattered across the cobbled setts. Passing these anachronistic modes of transport was quite nerve racking especially as it meant swerving across and riding between the tram lines.

Alongside would be the stomping hooves of a huge raw boned carthorse, while perhaps fast approaching from the rear, clanging and swaying, one of the large bogie cars of Manchester Corporation. Good fun, but it could be disastrous if your cycle wheels became caught in the tram lines.

Imagine a pair of schoolboys, talking in hushed tones as the minutes approached 9 o'clock, will it be another footballer to add to our list of cops? At that time the new batch of 'Sandringhams', named after football clubs, were appearing, some of them on the Great Central section, and almost invariably on the 9 o'clock. Sidings, usually full of vans, lay on the inside of the eastward curving main line and invariably concealed the approaching express until the very last moment. Steam would be shut off for the curve allowing the element of stealth and surprise to be perfectly realised. Suddenly it was there, wheel flanges screaming, towering, immense, and just as quickly gone, steam on, staccato exhaust for the last half mile into London Road. If there had

been a brass football in the centre of the middle splasher there might now be a little dance of ecstasy, for indeed the 'Sandringhams' were the greatest. No matter, that inept performance on the football field was the despair of our sports master, for this was the real sport, but so rare as to bring only the muted cheer of the spirit at the sight of a green boiler, the whirr of great driving wheels, the lunge and surge of pistons, coupling and connecting rods. The world was young and steam still king.

I remember the beginning of the first journey I made behind a 'Sandringham', a young lad of 14 years being packed off to spend a few days with friends of the family in Sheffield.

On arrival at London Road I walked the length of the platform alongside a magnificent train — or so it seemed to my unjaded eyes. Varnished teak carriages containing spotlessly clean compartments each upholstered in light browns and shades of gold. A fresh gentle perfume pervaded each coach and corridor, there was a refinement about the smell of polish in those days, the exterior of each carriage was completed by a final touch of magic in the form of a long nameboard, proclaiming to the intending passenger that he could be conveyed from Manchester (London Road) to Sheffield, Nottingham, Leicester and London (Marylebone). Even the 'Orient Express' couldn't have made me feel taller or more important.

The engine way out beyond the station canopy required rather more than a passing glance. This splendid looking machine gleamed in a coat of that loveliest shade of green, known as apple, fitting the 'Sandringhams' as no other colour would. It was the moment, minutes before departure, when a great express locomotive seemed at the nearest point to coming alive. No movement yet to be observed, except perhaps for a whisp of steam at the cylinders or safety valves, but the air around seemed vibrant, anticipating the imminent release of vast compressed energy, the quiet served only to emphasise the presence of vitality and life.

Eyes were feasted, consuming every detail. The proportions, from whatever the angle of view, were exactly right. The boiler, pitched high enough to suggest strength and power, but low enough to carry a nicely shaped line of boiler mountings. A running plate that turned gracefully upwards, in a shallow reverse curve behind the cylinders, then ran high and horizontal to reveal most of the 6ft 8in driving wheels, dropping in a much deeper reverse curve along the cab side to the level of the tender edge. The lilt and lift of this running plate suggested the girded loins of a racer, though there was still room for a generous display of driving wheel splashers. The outside steam pipes shaped like knuckles, combined with large cylinders and a complexity of valve gear, gave a great sense of forward thrust. I had never seen a steam locomotive with so many features juxtapositioned to suggest:

The swiftness of a racehorse
The power of a Hercules
The virility of an athlete

The whole was completed by a graceful nameplate, with raised letters assembled to make a name both regal and fitting — *Somerleyton Hall.*

Contact with the 'Sandringhams' continued for many years, especially on the Manchester-Sheffield line, until the lovely summer of 1958. This period of fond memory when I made a few, now cherished, afternoon visits to Sheffield Victoria. With 'Directors' right, left and centre, and the mid-afternoon crowned by the sight of a gently simmering, immaculate 'Sandringham' standing on the centre road between platform Nos 3 and 4 what more could one ask for?

A hectic half hour between 3 and 3.30pm with a B1 waiting to take out the 3.10 to Marylebone, and a 'Sandringham' for the 3.30 Harwich. Both trains would be hauled from Manchester, via Woodhead, by the mighty Co-Co electric locomotives, built especially for working over this huge hump. The change over from electric to steam traction at Victoria presenting the observer at the end of platform No 3 with a unique experience. The close comparison made even large steam locomotives seem positively lean and slender alongside the vast bulk of the electrics.

The presence of a 'Sandringham', especially with an East Anglian name, helped give credibility to the train it was about to take over. It was certainly hard to imagine a more incongruous setting for a 'Continental Boat Train', with its fictional overtones of romance and intrigue, than the heart of this great city of steel and industry. The old engine, though not too old even for such an important duty, would see the electric locomotive accelerate quickly away after uncoupling, then move sedately over the points to take out one of the last important express trains that her class was associated with.

Haunting the same East Anglian countryside traversed by the B17 and her boat train, were the last few survivors of the 1500 class 4-6-0. These engines, designated B12 in the LNER classification system, were the largest passenger locomotives built by the old Great Eastern Railway. With the North Eastern S3s (LNER B16) they claimed the distinction of being the last of the pre-Grouping 4-6-0s inherited by the LNER.

They were built at the end of the first decade of this century as an answer to the growing need for something more powerful than the 'Claud Hamilton' 4-4-0s though it says a great deal for the capacity of the 'Clauds' that the need had been deferred so long. The problem of weight and other restrictions, plus the requirement of high route availability, demanded that the new engine should be a comparative lightweight. The resultant low axle loading and a substantial increase in tractive power was the main reason for the varied interesting life the 1500s were to lead. One being the additions made to the class, long after the Grouping, for work in Scotland.

A dictionary definition of the word gorgeous says 'conspicuous by splendour of colours' that certainly fits the 1500s as first built, splendour of colour, coupled with grace and beauty of line. Visually they were the ultimate development of the 'Claud Hamiltons' ultimate, because it doesn't seem possible to imagine any further development of the theme.

An early lithograph in the December 1913 issue of *Railway Magazine* gives an idea of how the engines looked originally. It shows No 1505 in a rather dark royal blue, lined out in black and vermillion, with vermillion buffer beam and coupling rods. A bonus to all this magnificence came in the form of a most ornate, delicate tracery of brass lining, adding a glitter around coupling rod and coupled driving wheel splashers and cab windows. The whole being crowned by a brass chimney top. Indeed, a riot of colour giving much aesthetic pleasure to the fortunate enthusiasts of the time. Doubtless the present day economist would hold up his hands in horror at the degree beyond work requirement functionalism represented by this vision of beauty.

The 1500s had long life and many rebuilding variations which by degree caused something of their original charm and character to be lost especially in the large boilered variant. The aesthetic loss in the rebuildings by Gresley and Thompson being compensated by tremendous improvement in efficiency, a transformation, producing a locomotive to be compared with any modern 4-6-0 in the medium power range. This version, with its refinement of valve setting etc, became the most modern inside cylinder 4-6-0 ever to run on the railways of Britain, and the final survivors were, by something well over a decade, the last inside cylinder 4-6-0s to run in this country.

Contemporary with the 1500s, though a complete contrast in appearance were the North Eastern S3 4-6-0s, they were the largest class of 4-6-0 owned by that company.

Designated B16 by the LNER, they were probably the most successful mixed traffic 4-6-0 to come into the ownership of that company. The basic soundness of the design is shown by longevity, a factor which applied to most of Sir Vincent Raven's other designs. They lasted for around 40 years, both Gresley and Thompson considered them worthy of rebuilding, though in the end more than two thirds went to the scrap heap in their original condition. They rated among the most successful mixed traffic 4-6-0s ever built, for in a long life they performed with distinction every sort of goods, passenger and excursion working, even in old age they were still being used for the same type of duties they had been built for, the joints may have been creaking a little but I never saw them relegated to light or menial tasks. The B16s like their brawny muscular companions, the heavy gang of the old North Eastern, namely the J27 0-6-0s and Q6 0-8-0s survived to see many hundreds of Gresley's own engines fall first to the cutters torch. A tribute indeed to the sound engineering of Darlington Works.

Although the B12s and B16s were the last of the LNER pre-Grouping 4-6-0s they were really worlds apart. The regal splendour of the unrebuilt 1500s was a reminder of the antimacassars and crowded colour of a Victorian or Edwardian drawing room, the silhouette leaning back to a 19th century ancestry. The austere but ruggedly handsome B16s, with high pitched boiler and air of thrusting competence — well supported in practice, seemed to anticipate the shape of things to come, even in the last decade of steam these engines still looked remarkably modern.

The B1 class 4-6-0 produced by Gresley's successor, Thompson, was arguably the best thing

he did, for apart from being a good performer, and in this respect it equalled the Great Western 'Halls' and Stanier 5s, it retained the classic good looks of another age. The elegant line of boiler mountings included a robust looking but shapely chimney and nicely moulded dome. The running plate high enough to clear the coupled wheels, still allowed the boiler to sit snug without the 'turned up collar' appearance that beset some postwar standard types. These, in my view the most handsome locomotives to emerge from the last two decades of steam, served as atonement for the aesthetic mutilation suffered by some of the larger Gresley engines. Ultimately over 400 were built, providing a formidable barrier against the flood of Western and Stanierisation manifest in the visual appearance of the new standard types built for British Rail. LNER enthusiasts can thank him for helping to retain a North Eastern image in places where it should be, right to the end of steam.

In early 1947 I commuted daily from Levenshulme (midway between Manchester and Stockport) into Manchester arriving at London Road about 8.05am. The remainder of my travelling companions hunched with blinkered eyes towards the station entrance, most of them with the prospect of a long tedious day of toil ahead. My own moment of truth being deferred for I turned in the opposite direction towards the platform end, to view the engine and train of the 8.25 to Marylebone, already standing alongside platform A (now No 1 platform).

A train I had used frequently when travelling to Sheffield, riding behind many different types of locomotive, though none could claim to have excited me more than the Pacifics. I could never quite get used to leaving London Road behind one of these celebrated engines. They had an aristocratic air and a suggestion of apology was necessary for finding them on such a secondary main line. They may not have achieved such spectacular results here as on their own Great Northern stamping ground, but they did much to boost the LNER enthusiasts morale at London Road, especially when he was constantly reminded of the prestige and power of the LNERs great rival, in the form of 'Scots' and Stanier Pacifics.

By early 1947 the 8.25am had been discovered by the B1s — not quite a Pacific, though we platform enders inclined to think it at least the equal of Class 5s, 'Jubilees' and 'Patriots'. Brand new ex-works engines straight from Vulcan to Gorton were appearing on the train too, sometimes three in a week during the spring and early summer of that year, and even if their stay was brief they seemed to get a run on the 8.25am. This my first sighting en masse of the B1s was a revelation, the one or two seen in wartime black had not registered to anything like this degree. It required the early postwar decision of the LNER for a return to apple green, to reveal in the B1 a positive stunner, truly North Eastern in appearance, and quite magnificent. One imagines, had the Grouping not taken place, a continuing locomotive development at Darlington may ultimately have produced something like this. Though I claim allegiance to all things Great Central I never saw anything heading out of London Road that brought greater delight to the eye.

The period between mid-1946 and 1950 when I travelled frequently between Manchester and Sheffield can now be viewed retrospectively as one of the most interesting in the history of this very spectacular main line. It saw the advent of the B1s in large numbers, and the swan song of the remaining Great Central 4-6-0s, particularly the B7s on the Liverpool-Hull trains. The Pacifics and 'Green Arrows' were still in evidence though on a diminishing scale. Goods working was as varied as ever, so you could expect to see examples of all the remaining Great Central freight engines plus visitors from other areas and standard LNER classes.

Mentioning the B7s on the Liverpool-Hull's is a reminder of how these magnificent engines held their own until well within sight of the cutters torch. No menial tasks for them to work out their old age. I doubt if any other pre-Grouping mixed traffic 4-6-0 in the country at that time, 1946/7, dominated a passenger service to the extent that they did on the Liverpool-Hull's between Manchester and Sheffield.

Photographs, words, do not, cannot, give more than a glimpse of the sort of 'presence' exuded by the B7s. Standing spellbound beside them you felt that in length, height, width they filled the extremity of the loading gauge to bursting point. The boiler, which seemed almost visibly to swell under your gaze, was supported at the rear by a vast Belpaire firebox four square and almost toppling a quite substantial cab, appearing the more commodious for its double side windows. The smokebox door being typical of the later Robinson express engines, with its superior stare, and look of utter contempt for any gradient that may get in its way.

The lusty appearance of the engines was well supported in practice for the B7s were savage exciting engines to travel behind. With brute strength and great power they seemed to revel in the gradients of this most fearsome 40 miles of Great Central main line. Many a chilly evening in the year of 1946, I have joined the 5.25 from Manchester Central as passenger in the first coach. It was sometimes like the calm before a storm for though the weather in Manchester might be cold but quiet, there could be a complete transformation by the time you arrived in the hills. Thus many a wild winter's night as we climbed past the chain of reservoirs towards Woodhead, I have craned through an open window listening, face tingling with the cold, as one these magnificent engines rent the night asunder. Four cylinders roaring defiance at the gradient, the tiny chimney spitting a stream of red hot cinders towards the stars, the darkness occasionally flashed with white light as the fireman sweats and attends the firebox door. Superb pyrotechnics, the tape recorder's dream, yet the B1 did it with half the fuss and faster, and believe me it needed a pocket Hercules to cock such a snook at the B7s.

'No fuss and faster' could almost have been the clarion call of the B1s. Their job was to roam far and wide over most routes on the old LNER system and prove themselves that little bit better than the many different types they replaced. Quite a formidable task and one most ably carried out.

The Woodhead route between Manchester and Sheffield did not, to my knowledge, ever completely beat a locomotive type, but it tamed quite a few. Up to the coming of the B1s it was the ex-Great Central 4-6-0s and 'Directors' who could claim to have best mastered the long grind. The Pacifics and 'Green Arrows' were never, in my experience, very happy on this line, certainly you had to look elsewhere to find evidence of their quite legendary powers, in terms of performance. With the B1s it was an instant success story, no other passenger steam locomotive so completely dominated this formidable mountain backbone.

My first experience of riding behind a B1 over Woodhead happened one evening in 1947. I had been on a business trip to Sheffield, and arrived back at Sheffield Victoria, for the return to Manchester, with only seconds to spare. Not even enough time to sprint to the front end and identify the engine at the head of this substantial train of 10 or 11 bogies. The gradient starts virtually at the platform end, and continues as an unbroken climb for almost 20 miles up to those twin black holes with the awesome name, at an average of about 1 in 125. From the moment of go something at the front end had taken a firm grip, for the tugging was to some purpose. Travelling the line as often as I did, made one sensitive to small changes and, in broad terms, it didn't require a stop-watch to indicate an unusually energetic performance.

Curiosity now got the better, I threaded along yards of corridor across bucking, jerking end connections until finally I arrived in the almost empty first coach. It was a murky night but I opened the window to be confronted by the ghostly glow of carriage lights thrown back from cutting walls, or dancing eerily among the black branches of close up woodland. One thing was for sure, whatever witches brew had found its way into the water up front it wasn't contained in a Pacific or Prairie boiler, the sharp bark of the exhaust made that clear. It was a bark to some purpose too, rapid, confident, no suggestion of heavy labour. The intermittent glow from an opened firebox door reflected back and quickly lost in the overhead trail of richly aromatic smoke and steam. I reckoned speed was well into the 50s when I had to make a quick withdrawal of my head for the short but rather constricted Thurgoland Tunnel. The speed being held, perhaps slightly increasing as we approached the Penistone stop, here a quick glimpse showed a clean gleaming B1.

I had come up from Sheffield behind all sorts of engines in the last few years but no engine, with the possible exception of a 'Director', had shown such an unfussy easy grasp of its problems. The start out of Penistone is crucial, it could show skilled enginemanship, a good engine, or both. The gradient is heavy, (for a short distance 1 in 100 — the steepest bit on the line), there is a sharp curve and probably a greasy rail. With the old Great Central flat footers the drivers just opened the regulator and sat back, they may have plodded rather on level main lines but these old 4-6-0s, and the B7 was perhaps the best and pretty well had the measure of the Woodhead see-saw. I watched, anxiously — but there was no problem, we moved, albeit slowly, no trace of slip, clean crisp exhaust. Though Sir Nigel has, at least in my book, almost saintly qualities, I must admit that I never saw a Gresley engine make such an unflustered start from this much cursed spot.

The bit from here up to the tunnel was probably the most awkward part of the whole length between Marylebone and Manchester. There is no let up in the gradient, snake like curvature, and the weather, which could be quite calm at Sheffield, might be a howling gale with biting sleet. The greasy mist, on the night in question, did nothing to help, in fact everything, including the weight of a substantial train, was against the engine. The B1 coped as good as any and better than most, the acceleration out of Penistone was, as always, slow but very sure and confident. Now the B1 had to dip its unsullied head into the black murk of the Pennine hole, like pulling a dirty old knee length sock over a cleanly washed foot. Carriage windows had to be tightly closed, but even so the sulphurous fumes from this incredibly narrow bore (you could almost touch the tunnel walls from each side of the carriage) usually succeeded in penetrating.

Downhill from Dunford so we emerge from the tunnel like a bullet from a gun, streaking away past the Longdendale reservoirs, the water shimmering in the moonlight! You don't believe it? Well I tell you its like that in these northern hills, never be surprised at an abrupt change in atmospheric conditions between one end and the other of the pennine tunnels, I know, having seen it too often. The line clings fairly close, curving sinuously around these lovely stretches of water, a perfect example of a valley usually transformed for the better by the hand of man. Now the silvery light, dimly reflected along the B1s boiler and flat sides of cab and tender, is scintilatingly caught by the rapid oscillation of wheels, coupling rods and motion. An exhilarating stretch of line, beautifully aligned allowing speeds into the 60s. Here the B1 showed attributes other than the hill climbing ones, running freely, with just a whisp of steam to sustain high speed.

The brakes are on for Dinting curve before slowly crossing the hair raising viaduct over Dinting Vale. Brakes off now for a fast finish down past Guide Bridge and the huge complex of Beyer Peacock's, Belle Vue's Midland mpd, and the mighty ex-Great Central nerve centre at Gorton. Gorton, one could imagine the men and ghosts of another age rising to bow in homage to the modest little giant hauling my train. For years — decades even, they had struggled over their drawing boards to discover something with all the attributes of Thompson's masterpiece. Ironical that for all the varieties of 4-6-0 which were

the result of their cogitating they came nearest in a 4-4-0.

Perhaps the driver of the B1, with whom I chatted for a few minutes at London Road, should have a last word. I had been invited on to the footplate and listened while he extolled the virtues of his now gently simmering machine. 'Well! I've had 'em all, B7s, Footballers, Pacifics, 'Green Arrows', but this little chap beats the lot.' Then glancing across at the Stanier Class 5 at an adjacent platform. 'As good as anything they've got over there you know — and make no mistake what they've got is first class.'

By 1957/8, the last period when I travelled frequently between Manchester and Sheffield, the journey had become transformed. Huge electric locomotives had flattened the pennine pyramid in the same way that a later generation of super electrics would remove the rigour and legend of Shap. For a while decade Sheffield Victoria had the distinction of being the only large railway station in this country where it was possible to see a steam locomotive take over a passenger train from an electric locomotive

*Above:* Cambridge shed on 19 May 1957. Class B17 No 61634 *Hinchingbrooke*. An engine very familiar to the author during the mid-1930s now almost within sight of the cutter's torch yet still showing the sort of presence that suggests:
The swiftness of a racehorse.
The power of a Hercules.
The virility of an athlete. *Alan Blencowe*

*Above right:* Cambridge shed on 8 May 1955. Class B17 No 61600 *Sandringham*. *Alan Blencowe*

*Right:* Doncaster on 23 May 1958. Class B17 No 61635 *Milton* on the 4.35pm to March. *Raymond Keeley*

and vice versa. I don't think many observers of those days realised just how unique and short lived this most interesting manoeuvre would prove to be. Observations suggest the B1s had the lions share of these engine changes, the impression every time being how slender the steam engine appeared against the massive Co-Co electrics. Now they are all gone, engines, passenger service, even Victoria is now just a place of memories.

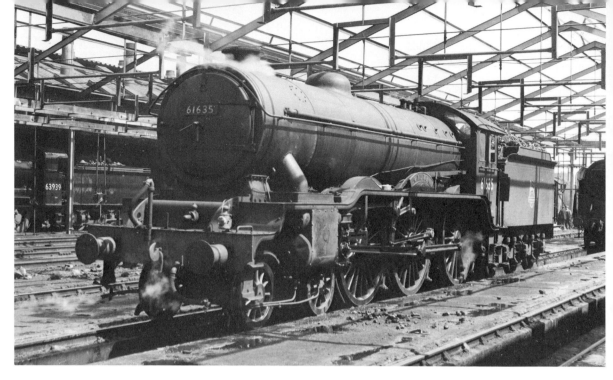

*Above:* Doncaster shed on 23 May 1958. Class B17 No 61635 *Milton.* *Raymond Keeley*

*Below:* Sheffield Victoria on 23 July 1958. Class B17 No 61641 *Gayton Hall* simmers gently while waiting to take out the 3.30pm 'Continental Boat Train'. The old engine had already seen a quarter century of life but was still considered good enough to be entrusted with such an important train. *Raymond Keeley*

*Above:* Cambridge on 3 October 1959. Class B17 No 61666 *Nottingham Forest* on a down local train. With only a few months of life left (withdrawn March 1960) but still looking every inch the express engine. The low side lighting clearly shows the bump of the brass football, what a pity one of them didn't survive into the preservation age. *Alan Blencowe*

*Below:* Cambridge shed on 23 June 1957. Class B2 No 61617 *Ford Castle*. The photograph clearly shows the appearance of the 'Sandringhams' after some of them were rebuilt by Edward Thompson in the early postwar period. The racy lines still remain, indeed the rebuilt B17s are a good example of Thompson rebuilding which harmonised well with the original. The ex-North Eastern tender, one time attached to Class C7 Atlantic No 736, will be noted. *Alan Blencowe*

*Above:* Sheffield Victoria on 5 July 1958. Not a double header. The B17 No 61641 *Gayton Hall*, which had backed down from Darnall shed coupled ahead of the B1, is about to move forward and then back on to the centre road between platforms Nos 3 and 4 prior to taking out the 3.30pm 'Continental Boat Train'. *Raymond Keeley*

*Centre left:* Down passenger train leaving Cambridge on 8 September 1957. Class B17 No 61626 *Brancepeth Castle*. *Alan Blencowe*

*Below left:* Cambridge shed on 16 June 1957. Class B17 No 61660 *Hull City*. *Alan Blencowe*

*Above right:* End of the line for a B17, No 61665 *Leicester City*, waiting to be scrapped at Doncaster Works. Photo taken on 10 May 1959. *Raymond Keeley*

*Right:* Class B12/3 No 61533 with afternoon Oxford-Cambridge passenger train near Itters Sidings about three miles west of Verney Junction on 28 September 1959. The girder bridge in the background carries the ex-Great Central main line. The very comfortable ex-LMS corridor coaches (mid-1930s vintage) will be noted. *Alan Blencowe*

*Left:* Cambridge shed on 13 April 1957. Class B12/3 No 61561.
*Alan Blencowe*

*Below left:* Down local passenger train leaving Cambridge on 22 September 1957. Class B12/3 No 61570.
*Alan Blencowe*

*Above:* Cambridge shed on 16 June 1957. Class B12/3 No 61570 and J20 0-6-0 No 64698.   *Alan Blencowe*

*Centre right:* Up goods passing Doncaster on 23 May 1958. Class B16 No 61430. At the time of the photograph the engine was still basically as built 37 years before, a tribute indeed to a sound locomotive design and the superb engineering practice of Darlington works.
*Raymond Keeley*

*Right:* Sheffield Victoria on 5 July 1961. Class B16/3 No 61449 on the 6.17pm train to Newcastle. The engine is shown as rebuilt by Thompson in 1944 with Walschaerts valve gear raised running plate etc.
*Raymond Keeley*

*Left:* A murky morning at Leeds City on 21 May 1958. Class B16 No 61429. *Raymond Keeley*

*Below left:* Sheffield Victoria on 6 July 1961. Class B1 No 61328 on a stopping train to Nottingham. *Raymond Keeley*

*Above:* The 12.15pm Marylebone-Manchester passing Woodhouse station on 19 August 1958. Class B1 No 61036 *Ralph Assheton*. *Raymond Keeley*

*Centre right:* Class B1 No 61183 passing Darnall with an up train on 23 August 1958. Note the coal in the tender piled high above the cab roof. *Alan Blencowe*

*Right:* Manchester Central on 17 September 1957. Class B1 No 61161 with the 5.35pm to Hull. *Raymond Keeley*

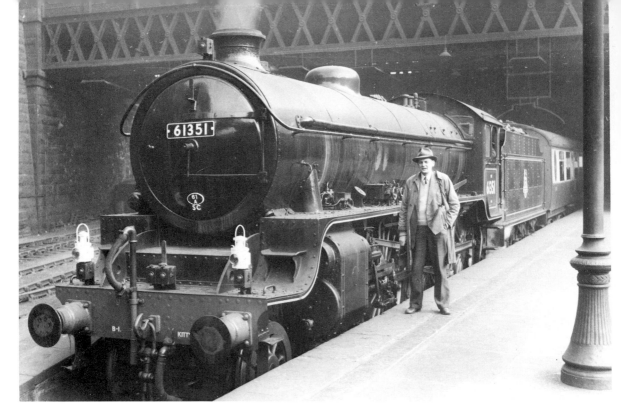

*Above:* Edinburgh train at Glasgow Queen Street on 23 May 1957. Since the engine, B1 class No 61351 recently ex-works, was a Kittybrewster loco (note shed plate and name on the buffer beam) this working may have been the first move in the long trek home. The gentleman in rough garb (elegance of dress was certainly not required on steam shed visits) is Alan Blencowe, friend and mentor of the author, and without whom so much would have remained undone. *Raymond Keeley*

*Below:* What a splendid impression of steam power and speed is conveyed by this photograph of Class B1 No 61190 hurrying north with a Kings Cross-Grimsby express. The location is near Everton signalbox just north of Sandy on the old Great Northern main line. The date is 17 August 1959. *Alan Blencowe*

*Above:* The 10.10am from York has just arrived at platform No 14 Manchester Victoria, 17 April 1959. Class B1 No 61084. The smokebox numbering is, to say the least, interesting! *Raymond Keeley*

*Below:* Sheffield Victoria on 19 May 1957. Class B1 No 61050 on an eastbound train. This and the following photograph clearly shows how the positioning of the smokebox hinge straps could influence the 'look' of a locomotive. Each time I see this photograph I think — pure Great Northern, what Ivatt might have done had he perhaps been 10 or 15 years younger and produced a post 1918 4-6-0 to augment his Atlantics! *Raymond Keeley*

*Above:* Sheffield Victoria on 4 March 1959. Class B1s Nos 61258 and 61306. Note the position of the hinge straps. *Raymond Keeley*

*Below:* Platform No 12 at Manchester Victoria on 14 September 1957. Class B1 No 61268 ready to leave with the 3.10pm Blackpool. The shed code (56A) denotes the home depot as Wakefield. *Raymond Keeley*

*Above:* Sheffield Victoria on 19 August 1958. Class B1 No 61159 simmers alongside D11 No 62661 *Gerard Powys Dewhurst.* *Raymond Keeley*

*Below:* By way of contrast to the previous photograph and in consequence of having mentioned them in the text, here is a picture of one of the giant electrics that whisked

comparatively lightweight trains over the Pennine gable at speeds far beyond anything steam could manage. Imagine the sensation, for those of us who experienced it initially, of climbing to Woodhead at something like the speed one normally experienced coming down. Even the Pacifics hardly challenged these engine for bulk and vastness of size. *Raymond Keeley*

*Above and below:* Mention of the magnificent B7s in the text prompted to search out a couple of prints showing these engines in LNER livery. Both photographer, whom I am indebted to, and location are unknown to me, but the photographs, particularly that of No 5473, capture something of their beefy impressive appearance. In my opinion no more striking mixed traffic 4-6-0 ever ran in Britain. I regularly curse myself for not having a satisfactory camera to record them on the many occasions I saw them leaving Manchester Central on the 5.35pm to Sheffield and Hull in late 1947/early 1948. *Raymond Keeley collection*

# Vintage Four Coupled

Vintage was the ripened beauty and aesthetic line of the old engines to be described, even though by the mid-1950s it lay concealed beneath a layer of dirt, grease, or rather dreary standardised livery. But peel off the skin of grime and dull colours, return their coat of many shades and tall they stand, revealed in a pristine glory of old. See the green and ochre transformation of *Butler-Henderson* and *Glen Douglas* and cry shame that the blue elegance of a 'Claud Hamilton' did not join them.

By the mid-1950s four coupled tender engines had been outmoded for decades though a surprisingly large number still remained. By the late 1950s those remaining in the one time areas of the LNER were either the supreme examples built by pre-Grouping companies, or those late developers the Class D49 'Hunts' and 'Shires'. The D49s, like their compatriots the Southern 'Schools' class, were a great locomotive class, but really they were no more than an eleventh hour extension of the type which had reached a zenith before the big four Grouping.

My first favourite among pre-Group 4-4-0s were the LNER Class D11s the 'Directors', my good fortune was seeing them when they were still running one of the best trains of the day on the Great Central section of the LNER. A few hundred yards' jaunt across the fields would bring me to a favoured lineside spot at about 7.45pm on many prewar summer evenings. I knew I could expect the sight of not only a 'Director' but also a different sort of masterpiece in delectable apple green. This one, though visually quite stunning, was bodily riddled with imperfections of which fortunately I was unaware, thus my hero worship of the magnificent 'Sam Fay' 4-6-0s continued unblemished.

The line northward from my spot is dead straight and on a rising gradient to Hyde Road station half a mile away, then curving east to Fairfield Junction. South it drops away in a cutting towards Levenshulme station and westward round the Manchester suburbs to Central station. Eyes scan north, ears tuned to sounds from the south, all quiet except for the distant whirr and clatter of a tramcar on Reddish Road. A new sound is caught, tiny sound waves of muffled pounding carry the message to straining ears. In a split second the eyes get the picture in the drift of smoke and steam to the south. Suddenly, bursting out of the cutting and under a road bridge, a brilliant green locomotive bursts into the narrow visual limits of my immediate world. This was the way to see a 'Sam Fay' at its best, working hard uphill, a strong mixture of smoke and steam spurting from the small chimney, any imperfections were not apparent under these conditions with the engine in full cry on a substantial Manchester-Leicester express. A stout boiler golden green in the low evening sun, flashing coupling rods appearing slightly disembodied you normally associated such a large engine with connecting rods and outside cylinders. As the 'Sam Fay' disappears from view beyond Hyde Road a streak of steam rapidly approaches from the east, the space between the distant platform awnings is suddenly filled by a black shape rapidly increasing in size as it hurtles toward the viewpoint, the slight roll suggesting the exhilaration of speed.

The engine, black and shining, is a 'Director'. The train, one of the elite of the day, the 3.20pm down Manchester from Marylebone and still entrusted to a 4-4-0. These engines had a handsome herculean look, even at the end of hours' sustained running you imagined them fresh enough to start all over again.

Little wonder to my youthful eyes the more slender looking 'Georges' and 'Precursors' seen at Longsight (my other haunt of those days) seemed small beer, especially when comparing their rather wet wheeze to the 'Directors' growl. I had yet to learn of all those legendary exploits on the old North Western main line. But although the 'Directors' never had the opportunity to provide posterity with evidence of hauling power to compare with the 'Georges' in their heyday I still regard them as the ultimate design of inside cylinder 4-4-0s from the Edwardian period. They looked and were massive, powerful, but not ungainly, like all the Robinson designs visual proportions were just right. Though this outward appearance of grace and elegance sometimes concealed less than perfect inner proportioning of firebox, boiler, cylinders etc, which, in varying degrees, remained an unresolved problem in all the large 4-6-0s that came from the Gorton drawing boards. All these splendid looking machines had plenty of muscle power but either in the wrong proportions, connected by weak sinew, or congested in some way. No criticism of Gorton design staff could be made in the case of the 'Directors' however, here they were bang on target whether it concerned appearance or efficiency.

Though only few in number the 'Directors' were still around in the late 1950s, a tribute indeed to soundness of design and construction. Now in old age and performing unexacting duties such as the stopping trains on the Manchester-Chester branch of the old Cheshire lines, the gentle meander through lush Cheshire countryside being akin to putting a racehorse out to grass. This relegating of express passenger locomotives to menial duties happened on many railways both pre- and post-Grouping, and particularly to 4-4-0s. A historical survey would probably show that as the wheel arrangement for express passenger locomotives developed the 4-4-0, somewhere in the middle of the cycle, most rapidly became obsolescent with the emergence of the modern 4-6-0.

By the time 'Directors' of Class D11 arrived on the Cheshire lines, 2-6-4Ts were about to take over and dmus were in the offing. A visit to Trafford Park shed in early 1958 showed the first ominous signs, No 62665 *Mons* stored and in a poor state externally. This is it, I thought, the end of the road for the 'Directors', I am glad my assumptions proved wrong. The curtain may have gone down on the last act but was about to rise on an exhilarating encore. By spring 1958 all except No 62663 (4IH, Stavely) were shedded at Darnall. Even No 62663 was seen regularly at Sheffield Victoria, where the remaining 10 were to work out a sort of Indian summer. In a brief blaze of glory they worked every sort of passenger train, none of which caused them embarrassment, not even the 10 or 11 coach trains of heavy corridor stock accepted from modern 4-6-0s or electric locomotives. My good fortune was to occasionally see them at work during this period, happily with a decent, though cumbersome, old bellows camera to hand.

There was one occasion of great pleasure during the late afternoon of a weekday business trip to Sheffield, when I accepted an invitation to the footplate of No 62670 *Marne*. The scene, the Manchester end of platform No 3 at Victoria, a briefcased city type wielded an incongruous addition to his uniform of commerce in the form of an elderly Ensign camera. The engine which the cold eye of a Ross lens was trying to record for posterity, trundled quietly in and out of the platforms on station pilot duty. Then, stopping for a few moments near the photographer, the driver, a real enthusiast as it turned out, looked down and with a smile said 'care to come up? — unless of course you are worried about getting a few specks on your white collar'! It needed no second invitation, I was on that grimy footplate in a flash, after all shirts can be washed and clothes cleaned, a golden opportunity like this does not happen every day.

Age expressed itself from every wheel, lever and knob on the footplate. Sheeting beginning to look like tin worn thin. Rust inevitably obtruded, rivet heads chipped and dented. Coupling rods, driving wheels — everything creaked and groaned. One imagined the old engine in youth several decades earlier, when no doubt cranks, pistons, axles moved like precision machinery, without rattle or complaint. The footplate would sparkle with water glass and brass framed dials to contrast with shining copper piping. Cab windows gleam in crystal clear, now chipped smoke stained like the view through a bleary eye. The external opulence of colour and majesty of line a focal point in any of the grey smoke racked caverns between Marylebone and London Road.

For a few memorable moments — minutes, I know not for time ceased to exist, we shunted back and forth, out over the Wicker Bridge back into the station. A seemingly aimless activity, yet with all the sense of thrill the child must feel on the fair ground roundabout. I felt like a small boy being given the piggy back ride by a favourite uncle. The humans on the footplate may have moved a lever or two and played around with a large shovel, but they were just flesh and blood puppets. The real 'presence' could be seen out beyond the cab front windows, puffing fussily about, pandering with courtly dignity to my pleasurable caprice.

Another occasion I managed a ride on a Saturday only seaside special as far as Retford. The train (Manchester-Skegness), 12 coaches of LNER bogie stock, hauled electrically as far as the Rotherwood change point. Here my luck was in, though judging by the external state of the waiting steam engine, other passengers may have considered theirs the opposite. A dark murky July day did nothing to improve the appearance of No 62668 *Jutland*. Indescribably dirty, steam escaping everywhere, rust bespattered, wheelspokes and running plate layered with grit and dust encumbered grease. The boiler had a 'splitting at the seams' look which seemed to characterise engines long out of the shops. Paintwork was rough, disintegrating, a catchment area for every speck of coal smut and dust. In short a not very encouraging sight. As the engine moved so it creaked a little, the long connecting rods causing a shudder of protest to pass through the crank pins and cranks to end finally in anguished squeaks from long suffering rails.

Finally, the transformation of ancient for modern was accomplished and we were away, not to any great purpose it must be admitted, for nowhere on this fairly flat stretch to Retford did speed rise above 45-50mph. The thick drift of smoke and steam that fell about the train did suggest that the engine was being thrashed a bit, and I suppose one could think 'shades of the 3.20 down Manchester' but that was 20 years before. For the moment it was just great to ride behind such a grand old veteran and see him still faithfully serving his public. The crowd, much larger than he could have expected in his days as an elite express locomotive, now came laden with all the baggage and paraphernalia of the seaside instead of bowler, brolly and briefcase.

A quick dash at Retford produced one photograph, reflecting (though I doubt that is the right word!) all the steam locomotive photographers'

problems — no sun for contrast, no shining paintwork to highlight just a little detail against the dim light of a grey day. One operates the shutter button and hopes for the best, especially when it might be an unrepeatable exposure of an old work horse enjoying a last gallop — or perhaps the word should be canter.

Though the few visits I made to Sheffield in that summer were pure joy, it still seems inexplicable that this small group of a generally outmoded type of locomotive should have this short reprieve, especially in view of the many hundreds of standard general utility types which were about. I have no doubt that an explanation could be found in what might be called accounting book reasoning. If this be the case then thank goodness our general slavishness to facts, figures and profit/loss columns is occasionally the cause of such a delightful and entirely unexpected happening. Of the 11 engines No 62664 was generally considered to be the best performer, at least by the drivers I spoke to. Maybe this was an omen, for *Princess Mary* was the only one to be named in the feminine, perhaps after all there is a heartbeat among all that steel and steam, though dimensionally they were supposed to be identical. Obviously the 'Directors' were better suited to the more rugged names carried by the remaining engines for they had the same massive appearance as Robinson's last designs of 4-6-0, to me, they represented locomotive masculinity. Now if asked to indicate their feminine opposites I would have no hesitation in pointing to the beautiful 'Claud Hamiltons' of the Great Eastern.

The 'Clauds' as the variants of LNER Class D16 were known, first saw the light of day early in the year 1900, and finally totalled 121 engines. For the next 50 years they were to haunt evocatively the whole of that part of the country known as East Anglia. Probably no other single class of 4-4-0 had ever dominated so completely such a large area of land. Basically this large segment of Britain is relatively flat so that nowhere did the 7ft drivers of the 'Clauds' have to contend with the sort of fearsome continuous gradients faced daily by the 'Directors' and North Western 4-4-0s in Pennine and Cumbrian hills. Despite this they had a compelling mastery of all tasks coming their way and regularly performed great feats of haulage and power output on the old Great Eastern main line.

The D16s though large powerful engines

especially in their rebuilt form, had a graceful almost dainty appearance. An assembly of exquisite curves commence with the head on view of the smokebox door's circular beading and hand rail, continues with a side view showing elegant curves of coupling rod and driving wheel splashers flowing gracefully into a superb cab completing the picture, in the same way the large curved bonnet framed the demure features of a lady in early Victorian times. The livery in early years was royal blue with red lining, plus liberal use of brass beading.

The success of the D16 as a class is not only proved by longevity, but in the long period of years over which they were built 1900-23, even this says nothing of the many rebuildings they enjoyed. I say enjoyed rather than endured, for most of the rebuilding not only improved efficiency but also appearance, a double not always achieved when an elderly engine sheds an old body for a new. I cannot think of any other 4-4-0 type in Britain which was involved in so many variations on the theme. Even the various marks of the famous 'Dunalastairs' were, in visual terms, no more than a gradual increase in the size of the original.

In the 'Clauds' the permutations seemed endless, from small boiler to large, flat chested smokeboxes, others presenting a pugilistic thrust, ornate coupling rod splashers or none at all, fireboxes round topped and Belpaire. The whole class was a constant delight to the enthusiast and a challenge to the cross referencing ingenuity of the collector of locomotive statistics. Everyone had fun ringing the changes including H. N. Gresley. Perhaps the high water mark of all the design variants came in the 'Super Clauds' of Class D16/2 as epitomised by Nos 8783 and 8787, these two engines painted green and with gleaming brasswork were for many years allocated to Royal Train duties. It is difficult to imagine more graceful contenders for the work. These, most famous of Great Eastern engines had long enough lives to become a legend in their own time, several achieved over 50 years of active life, a fact which does much to commend the basic soundness of the original design.

Would you believe that 30 odd years ago I could stand on a railway platform and hope the approaching train was headed by something different to the usual 'Claud'! That such a thought could be entertained (so unthinkable the context of now) is an illustration of the foibles of human

character, sometimes called contempt and usually caused by over familiarity.

I had been spending a few hours at March, visiting the locomotive depot in the afternoon, and the remainder of this November day in 1942 on the station platforms, where I awaited an early evening train to Peterborough. In the still air of a clear starlit night the gentle throb of aircraft engines could be heard, intermingling with these the distant sounds of movement from the marshalling yards and locomotive depot to the north-west. Dim slivers of light cast a fitful glow on the few blue and khaki clad figures and their tumble of equipment and kit bags. The yellowing illumination being just adequate to capture for a moment the cabside details of locomotives as they glided quietly out of the dark and were quickly lost again. The grimy, sometimes almost undecipherable number, usually revealed the identity of hardworking J17/19/20 class 0-6-0s, still the major workhorses in this eastern area.

Standing at the platform end, sufficiently far from the subdued lighting, the dark grips in enveloping mesh. There is an eerie sense of rolling flat country reaching deep into limitless East Anglia. Though even on the blackest night in Fenland the darkness never seems absolute, the rim of the horizon usually has just a suggestion of light as if at the edge of the world. One is aware of the quietness and yet of the clamour, the silence of night serving only to amplify tiny distant sounds which then collide with the nearby buffered clattering atmosphere, to bring magic to the far away sound of an engine whistle. The coming of morning light and sight will mufflle the ear, reducing the vastness of the unseen choir of night to the whisper of a daylight voice.

Out of the unknown, needle points of shuttered light and the eruption of a steam release valve herald the approach of my own train. The moment to quicken the pulse of any steam enthusiast — what would it be? A 'Claud'? There were quite a few about, though all sorts of unexpected things could appear in those days, that was the joy of it. In the event the engine that came striding ghost like with its huge 7ft drivers was a D13, a rebuild of a 2-4-0, and since there were only a few left quite a cop. A first glance would label it a 'Claud' but a closer look revealed the closed in coupling rod splashers and the single side window in the cab.

Choosing a decrepit ex-Great Eastern coach with a curious, half open half compartment arrangement,

I slumped in a seat to the sound of protesting springs, and began to study my notebook. What a haul, page after page of them, nowadays it reads like an inventory of treasures from antiquity.

Soon the little engine and half a dozen bogies were away over the flat lands towards Whittlesea. I walked around this elderly coach, of which I was the only occupant, listening to the creak of varnished timber door supports and the gentle tug of seating against the strain and stress of carriage framework, and marvelled. Marvelled that here for a few moments in time I had the landscape, the conveyance, and the motive power that had probably seen little change in a handful of decades. Well, it wasn't a D16 on the front but there were still plenty around and, to youthful eyes, a limitless future in which to see them, the D13s might all be gone tomorrow. Such is the essence and the weakness of nostalgia, the yearning for things passing beyond our grasp, and, possibly, an inherent awareness, sensation if you like, of our own immortality.

The LNER D49 class was, with the exception of the 'Schools' class on the Southern, the only completely new type of 4-4-0 to be produced by the post 1923 Grouping of companies which became known as the big four. Though both classes were contemporary, fortune favoured them in different ways, the Southern engine being an immediate success and though built for special duties eventually came near to eclipsing the legendary 'King Arthur' class 4-6-0s. Had Maunsell designed nothing else, his niche in the annals of locomotive history was assured by the 'Schools', where he achieved in the inner dimensions, a balance of working parts and thermal values that leaned to the sort of perfection Gresley arrived at in the A4s.

In outward visual dimensions both classes of 4-4-0 were similar, the Southern engine being fractionally the larger. The D49s, though magnificent looking machines, graceful of movement and beautifully balanced, were obviously not the apple of their designer's eye, clearly his sights were set in a different direction. Like the 'Sandringhams' they existed in a highly competitive world, they were to augment rather than replace, joining ranks with some of the great ones of the locomotive world like the North British, North Eastern and Great Northern Atlantics. Even the 'Schools' would have been hard pressed to shine in such company.

Working with the giants of the immediate pre-Grouping companies is not to suggest the D49s could replace them, it required something even greater in the form of the Gresley Pacifics to do that. But they were hard workers occasionally performing herculean feats of haulage in the absence of more suitable power, though doubtless there were embarrassing moments one of which I personally experienced.

The time, an early afternoon in 1944, I arrived at Glasgow Queen Street station bound for seven days' leave in Manchester — heading east to go south as only a railway enthusiast will. The train, a modest 10 coaches, probably with additions to come at Edinburgh, was prefaced, if such a contradictory term can be used when reading from the rear, by an ex-North British 0-6-2T. These stalwarts, podgy, powerful, were a familiar feature of the Queen Street buffer stop scene, some had spent their lifetime in this gloomy cavern. This one simmered peacefully enough, concealing, with deceptive calm, the tumult that would soon crack and burst the echoes in this hollow sound trap of glass and iron as it strode energetically between the platforms, nosing like an angry bull at the last carriage.

I walked the length of the platform — essential to see what delectable item of the locomotive designers' art graced the head end, there to be confronted not by the expected Pacific, but none other than No 249 *Aberdeenshire*. Dilemma, should I remain at the front and listen at close quarters to the D49 grappling with the bank, or return to a place in the last coach to observe the buffeting clamour of the 0-6-2T? I opted for the front, the coach was almost empty anyway, I could stand by the open window of the corridor door and almost touch the tender. Eventually a strangled shriek from the 4-4-0 was a signal echoed far away in this dome of non silence — the banker was ready and willing.

I can think of one or two daunting (for steam) exits from British main line stations, but none more so than Cowlairs incline. The gradient, at 1 in 43 is bad enough, what really made for the notoriety was the fact that the first 1,000yds or so of its fearsome one and a third miles is in tunnel.

We were away, the crisp exhaust of the D49 sounding briefly confident before plunging into the gloom. For a few moments I could hear the distant full throated roar of the 0-6-2T, strangely muted in the echo chamber beyond the fan shaped canopy. Then the trouble began. The 6ft 8in drivers of the

4-4-0 began to slip, recover, then slip again. In no time the first carriage was enveloped in smoke and steam, exciting for me, but I wouldn't like to think of the driver's comments. Progress thus continued, each 100yds of this comparatively short tunnel seemed endless. During momentary pauses in the furore at the front I could hear the gruff slow motion bellowing reverberating around the tunnel at the other end of the train. The anguish of the D49, as it painfully got a grip then almost immediately lost it, was like the cry of a wounded animal.

Eventually we found daylight and matters improved, the devil's cauldron of smoke and steam around the carriage dispersed and a more purposeful column of spent energy began to shoot from the 4-4-0s chimney. Thus, in more dignified fashion, as befits a 'Shire', did we reach Cowlairs station at the end of an ordeal — hard to know which of the two drivers would be more relieved! The remaining 30 odd miles to Edinburgh brought a return of honour to No 249, when very brisk running gave an on time arrival at Waverley. But one thing is quite certain, for a few brief moments (which at the time seemed interminable) in a dark tunnel a big 4-4-0 suffered the indignity of really becoming a 'passenger' locomotive!

The appearance of the D49s in the printed pages of practice and performance are few, just an occasional item here and there, giving a fleeting glimpse of the light that hides behind the bushel. By the middle 1930s the D49s, and they were not alone, were inevitably overshadowed by the tremendous exploits of their larger brethren on that great main line out of Kings Cross. Their working life was, in the main, confined to the areas of the one time North Eastern and North British Railways. This interesting aspect of LNER policy, the restricting of even modern types to a limited area of working, also happened to the 'Sandringhams', they worked mainly on the Great Eastern and Great Central sections. Only occasionally did the paths of these two important prewar engines cross, indeed they might almost have belonged to different railways. Even the two main variants of the D49s were largely separated. You had to visit the central lowland area of Scotland to see the bulk of the 'Shires', while the 'Hunts' could be seen all over Yorkshire, a situation to last throughout their lives.

How very different was life for the 'Schools' class which, though built to serve specific duties preclud-

ing the use of larger engines, soon came to rival those same 4-6-0s, and ultimately to become a legend in their own lifetime. Even the advent of Bulleid Pacifics and their eventual availability in large numbers did not oust this outstanding locomotive from main line duties.

The 'Schools' may have entered the realms of legend but destiny decreed otherwise for the 'Hunts' and 'Shires'. The wheel of fortune ensured they would always remain a secondary duty class, for an intermediate type of work. Indeed a lifetime to be worked out mainly in the shadows.

During World War II the D49s, like all engines large and small, famous and infamous, had a variety of jobs to perform. These were sometimes quite incongruous, Pacifics might turn up on a goods, an important passenger train come the way of a modest 0-6-0. They were halcyon years for the enthusiast and with a bit of luck presenting him with undreamed of opportunity for travel and observation. I particularly remember one journey made in 1941 if only for the variety of motive power that conveyed me over a comparatively short distance. The travel warrant said Manchester-Redcar and since route was not specified the options were open.

Problems ... should I travel Manchester-Leeds with the chance of a North Eastern Atlantic from Leeds to York? Hellifield-Kirby Stephen then across the northern Pennines to Darlington was tempting though the connections were awkward. The solution to this delightful dilemma was decided by the prospect of a Great Central 4-6-0 slogging over Woodhead. The Sheffield route it had to be, especially as the stretch between the steel town and York would have an almost non-stop interest, who could resist the temptation of Great Central 4-6-0s, 4-4-0s, Atlantics to say nothing of the Midland and North Eastern interest.

The route would be Sheffield-York-Darlington with a change of train at each place, and since you are probably wondering what all this has to do with a brief sketch of the D49s, I will skip the delights of the earlier part of the journey and get on to York where the D49 really comes into the picture. Sufficient for the moment to say that B2 No 5425 *City of Manchester* did battle with the Woodhead gradient. As the communiques of the day used to say 'our forces made slow but steady progress' amen to that, for the B2 certainly aroused the echoes of Longdendale on that day. Exciting stuff but long before the days of tape! A Great Northern Atlantic — surprise, surprise, brought my train into York.

The big station, crowded with all ranks and uniforms, navy blue, light blue, khaki — red tabs, 'erks' and gold braid. The atmosphere of the place, highly charged as usual, radiated its sense of momentous occasion for the multitude, suggesting the word destiny to be more appropriate than destination. From every direction a colourful feast of locomotives claimed attention. Jotting down numbers while balancing heavy kitbag and strapped around with shoulder kit, gas mask etc was no easy matter, but somehow everything was recorded.

Eventually a long train headed by a V2, apparently in trouble, curved around the platform. The 2-6-2 quickly uncoupled and was away to the sheds, leaving me to wonder what would happen now. The mental question didn't hang long, within a few minutes a pair of rather grimy locomotives came backing down on to the train. None other than D49 No 201 *The Bramham Moor* as train engine and a venerable Class C6 ex-North Eastern Atlantic No 702 acting as pilot. The Atlantic at 32 years of age, quite elderly for an express engine, was probably well past its best. Thick brown smoke curling from the chimney of each engine showed feverish efforts being made to prepare them for the task ahead.

Dragging myself away from the engines back to the train, I managed to find a corridor spot in the second coach. Jostle, shove, squeeze, with prods in the midriff from bayonet scabbard or water bottle, kit bags and big boots to trip over — no wonder the authorities pleaded 'is your journey really necessary?' Not to worry though, after all it was a vintage Great Northern coach, my armrest being formed by a brass window handrail inset with the legend ECJS!

A shrill whistle nearby, simultaneously repeated far down the platform were the signals to get this immense mass of boxed humanity on the move. *The Bramham Moor* lazily belched smoke and steam, while the Atlantic with thin high pitched wheeze slithered, paused momentarily, then tried again, the rather unexpectedly effeminate tenor voice from the chimney top loudly protesting. The curve was obviously finding somebody lightfooted. Gradually, to the accompaniment of an intermittent roar cum slip and a slow gruff puff, we moved at an agonising snail pace round the curve. Both engines were enveloped in a shroud of smoke from the midst of which every few moments there shot a column of steam attended by a squeal of anger — the Atlantic was certainly embarrassed. Even when the locos were well past the engine shed offices carriages continued to appear from under the station's fan shaped roof apron — however many were there, 17, 18, 19, well it was to be hoped the D49 was in good fettle. Gradually the two engines began to get a grip on this great train and we moved into the famous racing stretch, though not with any expectation of breaking records! Speed slowly gathered though it never became more than a jog trotting 50-55mph, you could hardly expect more with such a train and locomotives in a generally run down condition, the wonder was how some of them kept going at all. Once into the straight, the front end activity became somewhat obscured, but judging by the swathes of smoke falling around the carriages someone up there was working hard.

The stop at Northallerton brought considerable exit and entry of the passenger compliment, allowing a moment to nip on to the platform for a quick glance at the engines. The D49 seemed unruffled. The Atlantic — well if it is possible for a motionless locomotive to appear greatly agitated No 702 was giving a good demonstration. Safety valves, furiously blowing off, steam emerging from sundry wrong places in the lower regions, and a rattle of firing implements from the footplate.

We were away again, though not like the wind. I imagine the two engines made a wonderful lineside sight as they sweated smoke and steam at every seam in pent up, albeit wasteful, energy. Decades later the modern diesel would eat up the same miles at almost twice the pace, only a fraction of the fuss, but of course only half the load. Yet who wouldn't occasionally change the easy efficiency of modern traction for my journey of 30 odd years ago?

On arrival at Darlington I walked to the front stopping by No 201, the driver looked down, I glanced quizzically up saying 'grand engines the D49'. He looked hard at me then glanced at his sweating mate 'aye the D49s are grand engines but they should keep the likes of that b....... in front on coal trains. Well perhaps he was a Great Northern man, though we all get old and past our best even a North Eastern Atlantic. But how fallen are the mighty indeed.

The fates decreed the D49s should perform their

duties with distinction but largely in obscurity, so perhaps we could be forgiven any doubts about the capacity of these fine engines. They were never destined to shine on the main arteries but to operate those important cross country links that came into the category of semi-fasts. Maybe given different circumstances and opportunity the D49s could have shown the 'Schools' a thing or two after all!

*Below:* **Sheffield Victoria on 19 August 1958. Class D11 No 62664** *Princess Mary*. *Raymond Keeley*

*Bottom:* **Sheffield Victoria on 23 July 1958. Class D11 No 62666** *Zeebrugge* **with the 9.35am Lincoln train.** *Raymond Keeley*

*Right:* **Sheffield Victoria on 19 May 1957. Class D11 No 62670** *Marne* **ready to take out a train for Nottingham.** *Raymond Keeley*

*Below right:* **Woodhouse station on 23 July 1958. Class D11 No 62664** *Princess Mary* **on a Retford-Sheffield train.** *Raymond Keeley*

*Above:* Sheffield Victoria on 19 August 1958. Class D11 No 62666 *Zeebrugge* acting as station pilot. The B1 No 61036 *Ralph Assheton* is probably waiting to take over the 'South Yorkshireman' (11.36am ex-Sheffield) from one of the big electric locos. *Raymond Keeley*

*Below:* Early morning haze at Darnall shed. Class D11s, No 62667 *Somme* and No 62670 *Marne* in rear. *Raymond Keeley*

*Above:* Station pilot Class D11 No 62663 *Prince Albert* meanders across the Wicker bridge at the west end of Sheffield Victoria. Photo taken 23 July 1958. *Raymond Keeley*

*Below:* Class D11 No 62660 *Butler-Henderson* leaving Sheffield Victoria with the 9.42am to Lincoln on 11 September 1957. *Raymond Keeley*

*Above:* Woodhouse station on 23 July 1958. Class D11 No 62660 *Butler-Henderson* pauses with the 4.10pm Sheffield-Nottingham. *Raymond Keeley*

*Below:* Sheffield Victoria on 23 July 1958. Station pilot Class D11 No 62661 *Gerard Powys Dewhurst* pauses briefly between duties. *Raymond Keeley*

*Above:* Class D11 No 62667 *Somme* leaving Sheffield Victoria with the 5.49pm to Nottingham on 23 July 1958. *Raymond Keeley*

*Below:* The photographer's nightmare a gloomy day, a grimy engine, and, time being of the essence, a hastily 'snapped' photograph. The place, Retford, on 5 July 1958. Class D11 No 62668 *Jutland* on a Saturdays only Manchester-Mablethorpe train. *Raymond Keeley*

*Above:* End of the road for a 'Director'. Class D11 No 62665 *Mons* at Gorton on 21 May 1959, the dreaded white crosses are all too evident! *Raymond Keeley*

*Below:* Something of the winsome elegance of the 'Claud Hamiltons' is captured in this photograph of Class D16/3 No 62614 leaving Chatteris with a March-Cambridge local on 25 October 1954. *Alan Blencowe*

*Above:* Class D16/3 No 62562 standing in March station on 3 March 1955. *Alan Blencowe*

*Right:* Down fruit train standing at St Ives on 7 August 1956. Class D16/3 No 62589. *Alan Blencowe*

*Below:* Class D16/3 No 62597 finds rest in a quiet corner of the ex-Midland Railway's Spital shed at Peterborough. The engine at this date, 11 July 1959, was being employed on the Peterborough-Northampton services. *Alan Blencowe*

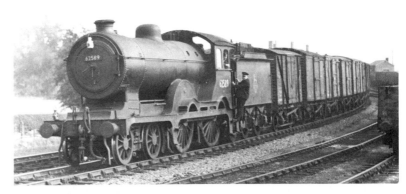

*Above:* Cambridge shed 7 July 1957. A watery sunshine reflects some of the attributes of a very graceful machine. D16/3 No 62618.   *Alan Blencowe*

*Below:* Down passenger train for York at Doncaster on 28 May 1958. Class D49/2 No 62754 *The Berkeley*. *Raymond Keeley*

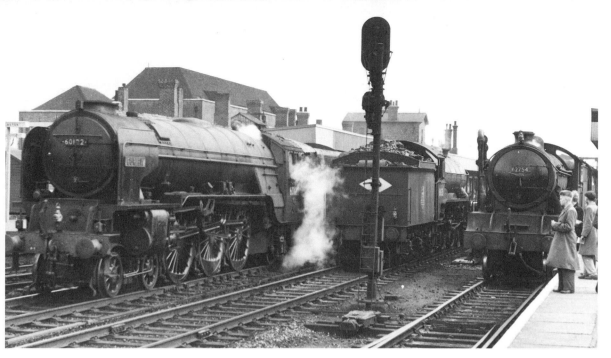

*Above:* Another view of No 62754 at Doncaster on 28 May 1958 alongside B17 No 61635 *Milton* and A1 class Pacific No 60122 *Curlew*. Getting the 4-6-2, 4-6-0 and 4-4-0 together in one shot perhaps makes for a rather unusual photograph. *Raymond Keeley*

*Below:* Scarborough shed on 22 May 1958. Class D49/2 *The Craven*. The photograph shows the rotary drive for the cam operated Lentz poppet valves. All 40 of the engines in Class D49/2 named after Hunts used this unusual valve gear. A unique situation I would think for a whole class to be built with one of its most vital mechanical parts representing such a radical departure from normal practice. But then it was typical of the boldness and unorthodoxy of Gresley. *Raymond Keeley*

*Left:* York on 31 August 1957. Class D49/2 No 62775 *The Tynedale* has just arrived with the 11.20am Doncaster-York. *Raymond Keeley*

*Centre left:* Selby shed on 31 August 1957. Class D49/1 No 62731 *Selkirkshire* moves cautiously on to the table under the watchful gaze of J39 0-6-0 No 64728 and Q6 0-8-0 No 63451. *Raymond Keeley*

*Below:* The east end of Leeds City station on 24 May 1957. A rather decrepit looking D49/2, doyen of the class No 62736 *The Bramham Moor*, stands at the head of a local passenger train. *Raymond Keeley*

*Right:* Darlington shed on 21 May 1958. Class D49/2 No 62765 *The Goathland* gleaming in ex-works condition, but the engine only had another 18 months of life. *Raymond Keeley*

*Below right:* Scarborough shed on 22 May 1958. Class D49/2 No 62767 *The Grove*. *Raymond Keeley*

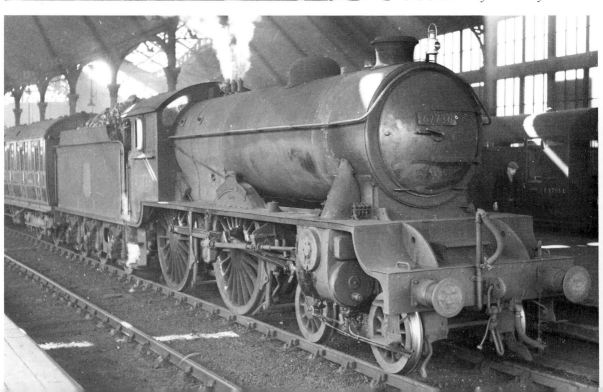

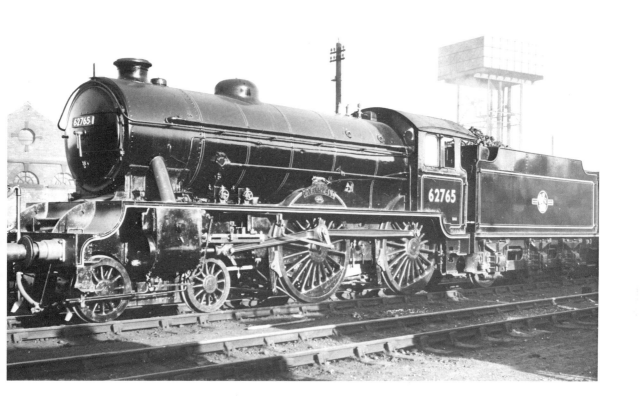

*Above left:* Scarborough shed on 22 May 1958. Class D49/2 No 62762 *The Fernie*. Clearly seen is the reverser shaft which through rotary movement passing via a series of bevel gears, shafts and spiral gears allowed movement of the camshaft transversely to the locomotive centreline. This allowed different sets of cams to operate against the poppet valves bringing variation in the cut off and, if required, reversal. *Alan Blencowe*

*Below left:* Sheffield Victoria on 5 July 1958. Class D49/1 *Nottinghamshire*. *Raymond Keeley*

*Above:* Thornton Junction shed on 22 May 1957. Class D49/1 No 62713 *Aberdeenshire*. *Alan Blencowe*

*Below:* The east end of Leeds City station on 23 May 1957. Class D49/2 No 62761 *The Derwent*, then only six months away from extinction, heads a local stopping train. *Raymond Keeley*

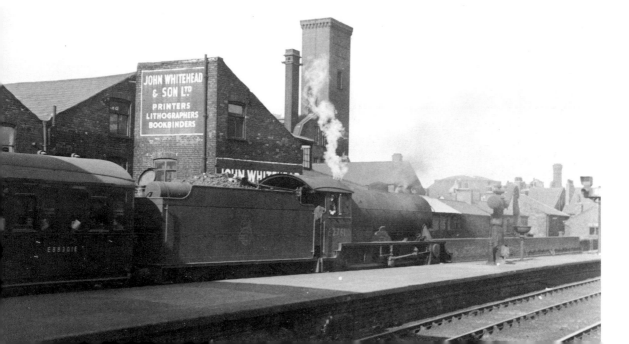

JOHN WHITEHEAD & SON LTD
PRINTERS
LITHOGRAPHERS
BOOKBINDERS

*Above:* Class D49/2 No 62767 *The Grove* reverses direction on the turntable at Scarborough. Taken on 22 May 1958. *Raymond Keeley*

*Below:* The end for a D49. No 62746 *The Middleton* awaits the hammer at Darlington Works on 22 May 1958. Note that the nameplate remains intact, one wonders how long it would have survived in such an exposed position 20 odd years later! *Raymond Keeley*

*Above right:* Since, in the text, the D49s have been compared with the Southern 'Schools' class, I thought it might be appropriate to include a couple of photographs of the latter class. This one of No 30913 *Christ's Hospital* at Stewarts Lane depot on 28 August 1958 clearly shows the sleek but formidable lines of these magnificent 4-4-0s. *Raymond Keeley*

*Below right:* Fratton shed (Portsmouth) on 28 August 1958, 'Schools' class No 30902 *Wellington*. *Raymond Keeley*

# Some Passenger Tank Engines

The last few years leading up to 1914 were a kind of watershed in the locomotive world, a period when late Victorian and Edwardian design was taken to its ultimate in size, not that sheer size of volume necessarily equates with efficiency. Inside cylinders and low running plates, items associated with earlier days, could still be seen incorporated into locomotives of enormously inflated size. Some large tank engines of the time serve to illustrate this backward view, albeit they were machines of superb presence and appearance, proving the highly developed aesthetic skills of many locomotive designers, even though internal dimensions may not have reflected the great advance external dimensions inferred.

Among the best examples of large pre-1914 tank engines, were the Great Central 4-6-2Ts of Robinson's design, which represented part of the final flowering of the Pacific type tank engine in Britain. They were not the ultimate in size among passenger tanks, that rather questionable distinction falling to the few 4-6-4T designs aspired to by some railways, but they were big and they did represent the final development of the passenger tank on the Great Central. The A5s, as they became classified by the LNER, had long lives and could be seen scattered around the areas of the original parent system for the whole of their years. Additions to their ranks were made after the Grouping specifically for working in the north-eastern area of the LNER, which might suggest they were superior in some way to their North-Eastern Railway counterparts, though to my knowledge this was never proved.

Building of the Great Central engines began in 1911 the year King George the Fifth came to the throne, therefore they became known as the 'Corona-tion' tanks. They were a most impressive and beautifully proportioned machine, but by 1958 they were held deep in the grip of old age. In this year I occasionally managed to photograph them at work around Manchester in a brief period of activity before their final demise. Briskness and vigour was still the order of the day, though I expect the joints were creaking a little. They now had a charmingly antique appearance which was understandable since they remained the only large, pre World War I tank engine, still working as originally built. Indeed some of them were getting on for 50 years of age.

Their last fling in the Manchester district was on the Marple-Macclesfield locals, for which purpose they were shedded at Gorton. It seemed incredible that the original Great Central batch had begun life nearly half a century before in the adjacent workshop. Born into an age so different in style and mood, (yet just about to pass into oblivion) they must have seemed the ultimate in suburban passenger power. Things had changed vastly by 1958 however, and at London Road station they were seen alongside modern, youthful looking 2-6-4Ts. The contrast did make them seem quite elderly. The Gorton shed staff must have had a soft spot for them because they were kept in fine condition, indeed meeting one of them at the buffer stops as you passed through the barrier at London Road was rather like being confronted by a frock coated gentleman from another age. The inside cylinders and low running plate helping to give an old world grace of movement, and dignity of bearing, which made interesting contrast to the bustling rakishness of the Stanier 2-6-4Ts with their outside cylinders and flashing motion. But the writing was on the wall for all, young and old, the banners of steam were folding everywhere, the dmus were already on the scene. On the Eastern Region's side of the station the steam locomotives found work only on the morning and evening rush hour trains and Saturday extras, for the rest of the day they could slumber peacefully in the depths of Gorton shed and perhaps consider — how fallen are the mighty!

There was something very special about the appearance of all the large passenger locomotives built by Robinson, an almost indefinable sense of refinement and breeding which pervaded even the smallest detail of their parts.

These qualities became highlighted when comparison was made with their contemporaries on some other railways. For me class always entered into it, a sort of 'Upstairs and Downstairs' if you like. Perhaps, if I stretch my imagination a little, it will help to further illuminate these ideas.

The great contemporaries of the Great Central A5s and 'Director' class 4-4-0s were the LNWR 'George the Fifths' and Bowen Cooke's 4-6-2T. Apart from being of the same wheel arrangement, there could not have been a greater contrast in the appearance of the four classes of locomotive. There was a drawing room elegance about the A5s and 'Directors' which remained even after the rust had set in. When performing the most mundane of duties, as for example the 'Directors' on occasional station pilot work at Sheffield in 1958, the blue blood always showed. It was rather like the country squire walking his estate in rough tweeds. But with their great contemporaries, the 'Georges', I always saw the cloth cap, knotted scarf image. They looked rough hewn and tough, with thick muscle and strong sinew. I intend no disrespect in saying this for something of the dignity of their labour showed through the spartan shape, and no doubt a coat of North Western black served to further emphasise the workmanlike appearance.

A consideration of one feature, the cab, will more particularly illustrate my impressions. In the North Western engines, both 4-4-0 and 4-6-2T, a simple shelter from the elements sufficed, in neither engine did this seem an integral part of the whole but rather a curved sheet on two uprights at the end of the firebox. In the Great Central engines the subtle curve of roof flowed inevitably into the cab side which contained neatly designed windows. In the A5, even the original version which did not have windows, the cab coal bunker and boiler fused in a harmony only rarely achieved in locomotive building. They were the proof that it was possible, though not easy, to avoid the sense that several dissimilar parts had been put together to form a whole.

London Road station was very much a northern terminus of the mighty London and North Western. The toe hold obtained by the Manchester, Sheffield and Lincolnshire and retained by the Great Central and LNER was never more than that. Three platforms squeezed to one side, the remaining three quarters of the station plus the adjacent Mayfield being the domain of the products of Crewe. It seemed ironical that the last pre-Grouping passenger engines to grace the portals of this one time bastion of the Premier Line's locomotives should be from the Great Central, for with the departure of the A5s went the last link with the joint station of old.

The last three or four years of the 1950s were really quite incredible, it was over 30 years since the Grouping yet locomotives of the old companies could still be seen in large areas of the country. For the Great Central enthusiast it was like a swan song, especially if you lived in the north Midlands, bringing something of the quality of a setting sun with the dying embers glowing brightly. The 'Directors' had closed ranks for their last, albeit short, period of activity around Sheffield, while in Manchester a few A5s adorned old London Road station with a distinguished, courtly elegance. Both of these elite classes, the supreme examples of the artistry of J. G. Robinson, being well supported by a host of lesser lights, for indeed the 04 2-8-0s, JII 0-6-0s, N5 0-6-2Ts etc, were still very much in evidence.

I had the good fortune at that time to possess a lineside permit, also the opportunity for some early morning photography around Romiley and Marple. The camera I used was rather cumbersome, though presenting nothing like the problems earlier photographers had to overcome, with their bulky cameras, glass plates etc. I sometimes look back to those foot slogging days of feverish activity 20 years ago and wonder — at the sense of urgency, the anxiety to get things recorded quickly. There seemed to be a subconscious realisation that the holocaust, which would consume steam, lurked around the next corner, and not at some distant time and place in the future. The few priceless negatives of hardworking A5s and DII, among other subjects, obtained shortly before the final oblivion, are perhaps the ultimate justification for all the sweat and toil.

Whenever I talk, or write, about A5s the word elegant keeps slipping in, though indeed it is only one of many agreeable attributes. One dictionary defines the word as meaning 'well formed in its parts, proportion and distribution'. There could be a a no more apt description of an A5, for it didn't really matter what angle you viewed these engines from there was still a majesty in their bearing. I believe they were the most elegant large tank engine produced in the pre-Grouping period. I would hasten to add, however, that other large tank engines of the time were not without their attraction, though their attributes lay in directions other than those described by the word elegant.

For the appearance of great strength and power you would look to the massive 4-6-4Ts designed by George Hughes for the Lancashire and Yorkshire Railway. If the search was for sheer, awe inspiring size, then pause before Robert Whitelegg's masterpiece, the huge Baltic tanks that he designed for the Glasgow and South Western Railway. They were very big and yet designed and embellished with such loving care as to endow them with the greatest beauty. Perhaps the lines of a racer are the consideration, then set your sights on the Brighton 4-6-4Ts for no other engines portrayed fleetness of foot better than they did, indeed it was a necessity for engines so indelibly linked with the 'Belle'. But when it came to 'expressing oneself with propriety and grace' (another dictionary definition) then the A5s had the edge on all others.

Unlike the solitary Great Central design the North Eastern Railway produced three designs of Pacific tank, though the last (LNER Class A8) was originally built as a 4-4-4T, the class being rebuilt with the extra coupled driver in the early 1930s. Like many older classes, particularly on the LNER and Southern they were affected by a policy that inclined towards keeping some pre-Group classes confined to the areas of the old parent company. The North Eastern Railway was a case in point, except for the B16 class 4-6-0s which did wander a little, you had to travel to Yorkshire and especially County Durham if you wished to see the locomotives of this old company in large numbers.

It was this situation, which still remained even in the late 1950s, that persuaded two colleagues and myself to spend a few days during 1958 in the north-east. We were richly rewarded, since not only was there a wealth of freight train working in the Newcastle, Sunderland, Middlesbrough area, but here, working out their twilight years, were the last survivors of that family of Pacific tank.

Some of the locomotive depots in this area appeared captured in a moment of time, as if it had frozen half a century back when a pre-Grouping pre-1914 atmosphere prevailed. It was quite uncanny. Each prospect of structure or content was like the view of an ancient sepia photograph sprung to life. The sensation was that of discovering buried treasure, with each shed or roundhouse containing jewels beyond compare. Although this was 1958 there hardly seemed any indication of the passing years, the half century might have slipped in time and not been noticed. The scenes were almost completely dominated by North Eastern locomotives, with the magnificent Q7 0-8-0s ably assisted by Q6 0-8-0s, J26/27 0-6-0s representing the goods motive power, and much of the local passenger work still being handled by the A8s and the much smaller G5 0-4-4Ts.

I suppose the last word that could be used to describe a locomotive built by Vincent Raven would be ostentatious, none of them attempted to cut a dash, or turn your head with beguiling line, curve, or adornment. But they were handsome in a rugged sort of way, and the competent appearance was well borne out in practice. This was entirely as it should be for I doubt if the average Tyne/Teesider, so long associated with the hard industries of coal and iron, would want to live with anything that suggested too much fuss or frivolity. So it was appropriate that his railway, and after all the North Eastern was basically a Geordie line, should reflect in its locomotives the toughness and sweat of that land.

The Pacific tanks certainly reflected the right image with their huge uncompromising slab sided water tanks and coal bunker. A small aperture cut out of these square yards of flat metal served as a lookout for the crew, making what must have been a rather dark footplate, though I expect the extra area of metal protection would be a boon when a cutting east wind blew. The running plate was low, and dead straight, no alluring curves there. But despite the almost deliberate squareness the result was not unpleasing, at least it made a perfect match for a landscape of dockland, pit shaft and bleak rocky coastline.

Both Great Central and North Eastern 4-6-2Ts, had long lives which was unusual for these rather large, obsolescent types of passenger locomotive, especially as most of their contemporaries, which includes the several types of 4-6-4T built by some railways (though not by any of the LNER constituents) had been ousted by legions of modern 2-6-2 and 2-6-4Ts in the 1930s and 1940s. When built they were considered by their Edwardian designers to be the last word in heavy suburban passenger motive power, and it really was remarkable, they lasted until the dawn of the diesel age.

The immediate predecessors of the A5 tanks on the suburban services out of Manchester's London Road station were, by comparison, quite diminutive, Small in stature but great in heart, you could call them Atlantic tanks which at least is a match for their heroic qualities. It was here, in the 1950s, that these elderly Great Central 4-4-2Ts (LNER Class C13/14) had their last great opportunity to display their talents. They were already an anachronism, being around 50 years old or more and near the end of a very long life. You would have expected such venerable old gentlemen of the locomotive world to spend their last few years just pottering about with a couple of coaches on push and pull (more anon of the one or two that did). They were, however, destined to leave this world in a much brighter blaze of glory.

There was an incongruity about London Road in the 1950s, at least in respect of motive power. In the London Midland section of the station, which was the major portion, you could, during the course of a day, see representatives of almost all the ex-LMS passenger engines from Class 4 to 8P, the suburban work being in the main handled by modern 2-6-4Ts. On the Eastern Region side, with only three platforms, most local services to Marple, Hayfield and Macclesfield were operated, in the main, at least up to the middle 1950s, by the above mentioned aged band of Atlantic tanks. In contrast, the main line trains to Sheffield were being hauled by the most modern and powerful electric locomotives this country had ever seen.

If the imagination is stretched a little the character and personality of a locomotive may be seen in the face on the smokebox door. An invention of the mind of course, and therefore particular to the person, the strap hinges, fastening lugs and handles, shape of the door, bulbous or flat, and the chimney, all helped the illusion that turned dead metal into living expression. The C13/14s always seemed to me to have a timid elderly look, I could

never imagine them being young. A complete deception, for once they were on the move they showed a sort of energy and elan on the local services out of London Road quite unequalled in steam days at that place. The phrase 'wolf in sheeps clothing' could never be more appropriate. The briskness and vigour invariably demonstratesd in their acceleration out of the Manchester terminus, always came as a surprise, indeed the present day dmus would be hard pressed to equal it.

The competition these little engines had to face was quite formidable, usually coming in the form of modern 2-6-4Ts the oldest of which, being a good quarter century younger than the Great Central engines. The most severe rivalry came from the Stanier 2-6-4Ts — probably the best modern large passenger tank ever to run in Britain. The rivals ran parallel to each other for approximately one mile to Ardwick Junction where the ex-LNER lines branched eastward. From the very low platforms of Ardwick station I have watched many times, transfixed, as a C13 comes galloping, lurching towards the viewpoint. The mask of deceptive timidity is down, a furore of belching smoke and steam urges the locomotive, with screaming protest, to change direction into the curve. Gallop is the right word as coupling rods whirl and disappear somewhere beneath the side tanks with each revolution. There is an illusion of huge driving wheels, indeed one had the impression of seven footers spinning round, though in reality they were only 5ft 7in. A further attribute, which helped transform their appearance when in motion, became apparent in the deep throated bark — Whoof whoof — Whoof whoof etc, which probably helped bring dismay to the big, purring, Stanier tank, who might have expected the rather ancient old gentleman with the big chimney, leaving from a couple of platforms away, to be quite out of the running.

By the end of 1957 the writing was on the wall, old age catches up sooner or later, now it was the turn of the C13/14 to face oblivion. Their duties on the suburban services out of London Road gradually being taken over by the much larger A5 4-6-2Ts and the modern L1 class 2-6-4Ts. Irony being added to the situation by the drafting of some of the ex-LMS Fowler 2-6-4Ts on to the erstwhile Great Central services.

However one or two of the C14s did manage to hold on at Gorton, for working the Oldham, Ashton and Guide Bridge service until this ceased operation. I made several journeys during the last few weeks of its existence. Indeed it seemed a miracle that the service had lasted so long, the traffic was sparse, the stations inconveniently placed and very ancient. The whole seemed like an incredible hangover from a bygone distant age — stations, engines, rolling stock. Even the tickets, right up to the last day, carried a legend that hardly related to the age of British Railways. Time on the OAGB appeared almost to have slipped a half century.

The station at Oldham, lying some distance from the bright lights of the town centre, was reached by traversing the dimly lit quarter mile of Clegg Street. A forbidding doorway did little to encourage the would be traveller to enter the cheerless interior with its flickering gaslight. The ticket clerk, warm and barricaded against this grim exterior, peered through his tiny pigeon hole — surprised perhaps at this venturing mortal. The old station heavy with age, careworn, uncared for, awaiting the sledgehammer's assault. Dusty well trodden stairways, the soot and grit of ages past, deep inset in splitting timbers, or ingrained in crevice or inaccessible corner. Ironwork, the handhold of generations, with pitted but polished shine, thickened with the paint of years, chipped here and there to expose a strata of layered colours leading the eye to a rusting iron core. Large cumbersome waiting room doors — did they, I wonder, contain more solid wood than finds its way into flimsy built small villas of today? Massive metal hinges of battleship proportions. Interior, a yellowed shadowy cavern, like a grey stained schoolroom from Dickens. Uneven smooth edged stone flags carry the footsteps to the gnarled knobbled exterior of the slightly sagging weary old carriage. The opened door reveals a faded cosy almost intimate compartment, plushy, musty, like the smell of old furniture.

A picture of creaking old age! Yet there was character, atmosphere, steamy and snug in the winter. Now, at Loughboro, Bridgnorth, Alresford, and a host of other places, we seek to recapture a non plastic era discarded so casually, scornfully in a thousand places now forgotten, the once red spots on the ordinance maps of yesteryear.

Earlier mention of the L1s reminds me that their brief period on locals from London Road before the dmus took over, was the only real contact I had with with engines. Compared with the ex-Great Central engines and even the Fowler 2-6-4Ts they seemed,

at least in my experience, inclined to be sluggish. Despite their small driving wheels and high tractive effort they didn't have the zip when getting away from stops so ably demonstrated by the ancient C13/14s in their last years. Perhaps the problem was high power combined with poor adhesion, high tractive effort is of little use unless it can be applied where it matters — on the rail.

Whatever problems may have been caused by lack of balance in the power unit, there was certainly no question of disharmony when the locomotives were viewed aesthetically. They were, in the writer's opinion, the most handsome large tank engine to emerge from the postwar period and had a distinctly Great Northern look. The very attractive profile, which could be said to be shared by the B1s, comprised a neat modern chimney, well shaped dome, and one of the best looking cabs ever placed upon a tank locomotive. The cab is the one feature that sometimes lets down the appearance of many, otherwise handsome, tank engines. Not so with the L1s whose cabs were graced by large well proportioned double side windows and pleasing arched roof. Ironically it is Edward Thompson to whom we are indebted for allowing this Great Northern appearance (particularly noticeable in the L1/B1s with smokebox door strap hinges set close together) to continue right to the end of steam. Hence the question arises, how could he have allowed those ghastly visual alterations to No 4470 — alas we will never know the true answer.

The Great Northern Atlantics were without a doubt the last celebrated locomotives of the type in Britain. Winners both in performance and looks, they became and remain a legend. Extrovert, flamboyant, jaunty — features so well captured on posters, on the front cover of *Wonder Book of Railways* and countless times in the world of railway literature. Monarch on the East Coast route well into the Pacific age and even then not easily dislodged from the throne. 'And what' you may ask 'has this to do with tank engines?'. Well, as a contrast everything, for the Great Northern also produced another Atlantic, a tank engine. A quiet unobtrusive little fellow not to be mentioned in the same breath as his larger brothers of enviable reputation. They were, to my eyes, quite endearingly feeble. The visual weakness was due to a number of things, a small boiler pitched rather low between the side tanks, a receding smokebox, which didn't help by bedding down into the frames like a face without chin or neck, and a rather long thin chimney. But it was the voice that hoarsely whispered from the latter that finally capped everything, thin, nasal, sounding uncannily like some poor human suffering from acute bronchitis. Appearances however are sometimes quite deceptive, for in reality these little engines were strong, comparatively powerful, and quite spritely, they certainly nipped in and out of Manchester Central more like two-year olds than 50.

The special affection I have for the C12s dates back 30 odd years, to interludes in wartime which are now a cherished part of memory. These happened during a few weeks in 1942 when I was stationed with a fighter squadron at Wittering in Northamptonshire. Occasionally, in a free period, I would hitch the couple of miles up the great north road to Stamford. Shortly before entering the town I turned off the main road to step through the portals of a graceful old world building. Striding into this place had the strange effect of having entered into a different dimension of time, as if the one great barrier that bedevils and confuses man had for a moment been torn aside.

The stonework entrance, which the imagination had momentarily endowed with magic properties, carried a modest little signboard indicating this to be Stamford East railway station. It did nothing to prepare the visitor for the tiny but exquisite booking hall and train shed within, terminus of the short branch line connecting the old town with the Great Northern main line. Indeed on entering the small booking hall you might well be sufficiently caught with the time slip idea as to expect a confronting of frock coated gentlemen sporting the tall stovepipe headgear of a quite different age.

The branch engine, a C12 of course, and looking rather bent with age, would be fussing importantly at the head of a short rake of faded teak carriages. Interiors had a slightly threadbare dusty look with overtones of one time opulence, exactly the way I remembered the, Sundays only, front parlours of great aunts and grandmas with their impression of elaboration, moth eaten velvet and round buttoned upholstery. Grey marked sepia photographs above the head rests might show a sylvan scene, or long skirted and straw boatered crowds grasping the joys of pier or promenade. If the ancient lineage of the wood beaded, brass handled carriages was not immediately recognisable, then the raised letters

GNR on the axle boxes were sufficient to complete the illusion of having stepped, Alice like, through the looking glass.

A journey of about three miles past quiet fields and hedgerow brought the branch train to Essendine, on the famous racing stretch of the old Great Northern main line. Essendine, an example of those magnificent country railway stations, the legacy of a greater railway age, which could at one time be found up and down the country. Sometimes they seemed set down in the middle of nowhere, but usually contained all the paraphernalia of the old time railway, large spacious island platforms, each provided with its own waiting rooms and other offices and accommodation, trollies, bay platforms and an abundance of staff, for the railway of those days was fairly labour intensive. By 1942 I imagine the facilities had become in excess of requirements, a way of life was beginning to change and, sadly, would never be the same again. However it provided an idyllic spot for a railway enthusiast, in the middle of a war, and a perfect antidote to the strain of service life.

As a vantage point, the station had everything in its favour, branch activity to give a localised personal heart beat to its life, and a place for a remoter sort of glory of great locomotives in full cry, compressed power expelled in vertical columns of smoke and steam to fall about station and train in long drifting swathes. I might read the experts analysing cut off or drawbar horsepower, but on these platform occasions emotion takes over from intellect as the sight of Pacific or Prairie charging Stoke bank, with perhaps 20 coaches swaying behind, caresses the excited antennae of the senses. The sound, distantly muted at first, reaches towards a crescendo, overwhelms the dumbfounded onlooker. Every thrust of connecting rod, every revolution of coupling rod and driving wheels, brought a tremendous feeling of unleashed power, so audible, so visible. Coming down they streaked, the approach was smooth, more like the low rumble of distant thunder, then a massive drum roll through the station. Probably between 60 and 70 though imagination nudged you to believe it more like 90mph.

I am supposed to be writing about Atlantic tanks however, so let us hasten back to the branch platform where the C12 will be gently simmering at the head of its train. A complete pre-Grouping assembly, red plush interior, all spotlessly clean, though I may be the only passenger. The contrast to the main line activity couldn't be greater, the haste and urgency of war now seems far away, reminding the watcher of a more leisurely, perhaps saner, way of life.

Finally the little tank engine, with apologetic asthmatic voice, moves away at a gentle lilting pace and is soon amidst fields of cows. There is the brief illusion of slipping into a century past as timeless rural England envelopes the branch train. The pause at Ryhall, the only intermediate station, is an eternal moment of distant animal sounds, of peace. The voice of the country railwayman gently bids intending passengers to join the train for Stamford. The guard views an imposing timepiece, beflagged hand poised ready. There is a reassuring sense of importance for unimportant things. Quiet leisurely words emphasise a sense of values slipping away. Even the gentle wheeze from the engine is a protest at the indecent haste of so called progress, a regret for the passing of an age, matching dreams of a

world without clamour or discord. How could I fail to love for evermore this long funnelled little fellow of the slightly comic countenance.

But such idyllic moments are brief in the timetable of life, swiftly passing to be replaced, on this occasion, by the ominous sound of night flying and the engines of war.

*Right:* **Sheffield Victoria on 23 July 1958. Class C13 No 67439 on the 9.30am local train from Chesterfield. On the date of this photograph the engine would be an incredible 53 years of age, but only a few months away from the old bones being laid to rest, withdrawal being in November 1958.** *Raymond Keeley*

*Below right:* **Reddish North on 15 June 1957. Class C13 No 67437 on a midday local from Manchester London Road to Hayfield.** *Raymond Keeley*

*Below:* **On a cold and frosty morning. Oldham Clegg Street at 9.15am 10 January 1959. No 67417, the last survivor of Class C13, on a local from Ashton. The dilapidated state of the station roof awning, (not long to survive) will be noted.** *Raymond Keeley*

*Above:* Gorton shed on 9 March 1958 Class C13 No 67421, this one of the two engines then regularly used on the Oldham, Ashton and Guide Bridge push pull services. The vacuum gear for the remote control of the push pull operation can be seen to the right of the smokebox. *Raymond Keeley*

*Below:* 12.15pm SO Manchester London Road-Macclesfield train arriving at High Lane station on 25 May 1957. Class C13 No 67444. *Raymond Keeley*

*Above:* Hayfield on 15 June 1957. Class C13 No 67437 having brought in a SO local from Manchester is proceeding to run round the train. *Raymond Keeley*

*Below:* Class C13 No 67417 on the 8.57am Guide Bridge-Oldham Clegg Street approaching the latter station on 4 April 1959. *Raymond Keeley*

*Above left:* On the last day of operation on the Oldham, Ashton and Guide Bridge service, 2 May 1959, Class C13 No 67417 runs into Dukinfield from the Stalybridge direction on an early morning train. The author's briefcase, hastily placed down while adjusting a temperamental camera, has contrived to enter the picture! *Raymond Keeley*

*Below left:* Oldham's Clegg Street station around midday on 2 May 1959. Class C13 No 67417 running round train, which by this time had been strengthened to, if memory serves me right, four coaches. In the background can be seen the platforms of Oldham Central station on the ex-Lancashire and Yorkshire branch from Manchester

Victoria. Evidence that stations existed at this place reveals itself only to the discerning eye of the railway archaeologist! *Raymond Keeley*

*Above:* The fatal X marks the spot! Class C14 No 67440 awaits her fate at Gorton on 28 July 1957, (works in the background). These engines differed only slightly from the C13s, mainly in the slightly larger side tank capacity and coal bunkers. *Raymond Keeley*

*Below:* The end indeed. Class C13 No 67419 being reduced to scrap at Gorton on 28 July 1957. *Raymond Keeley*

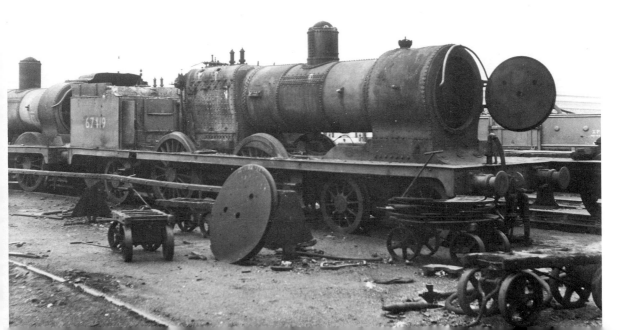

*Above left:* Pause between duties for Class L1 No 67782. Manchester London Road station in June 1959. *Raymond Keeley*

*Below left:* Guide Bridge on 2 May 1959. Class L1 No 67782 on the 12.25pm Manchester London Road-Hayfield train. *Raymond Keeley*

*Above:* Class L1 No 67798 leaving Reddish North station on 13 June 1959 with the 12.10pm Manchester London Road to Macclesfield. *Raymond Keeley*

*Above:* Class L1 No 67798 climbing towards Romiley with the 7.30am Manchester London Road (via Bredbury)-Marple Rose Hill on 14 June 1958. *Raymond Keeley*

*Below:* Marple Wharf Junction on 3 May 1958. Class L1 on the 1.0pm Manchester London Road-Hayfield train. *Raymond Keeley*

*Above:* Marple Rose Hill on 4 July 1957. Class L1 No 67781 on the 12.56pm Manchester London Road to Macclesfield. *Raymond Keeley*

*Below:* Peterborough on 10 March 1956. Class C12 No 67365 running light near Walton. The engine normally worked the Stamford-Essendine branch and, presumably, would be heading for New England depot, perhaps for a routine maintenance that could not be accommodated with the facilities of the small sub shed at Stamford. *Alan Blencowe*

*Above right:* Peterborough North on 6 August 1956. Class C12 No 67376 on station pilot duties. *Alan Blencowe*

*Below right:* Peterborough North (north end) Class C12 No 67398 on station pilot/banking duties. Particularly noticeable in this photograph is the large dome which, by giving a rather hump backed appearance, did nothing to help the rather endearingly feeble looks of these little tank engines. *Alan Blencowe*

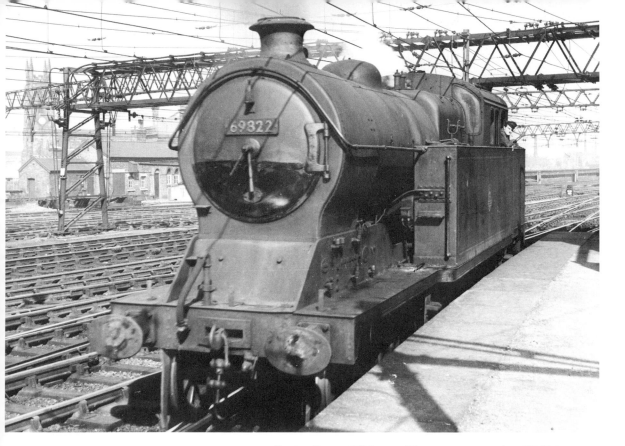

*Left:* Manchester London Road station on 4 June 1958. Class A5 No 69801 on the 7.30am stopping train to Marple. *Raymond Keeley*

*Above:* London Road station again on 4 June 1958. Class A5 No 69822 ready for duty. Since the time on the church clock shows 5.25 the engine may well have been taking out the 5.33pm to Marple. This was often a bunker first job. *Raymond Keeley*

*Centre right:* London Road station on 8 July 1958. Class A5 No 69801 awaits a further duty. In the background Class J11 0-6-0 No 64310 shunts vans on the lines leading to the adjacent goods depot. *Raymond Keeley*

*Below right:* On 7 July 1958, Class A5 No 69817 on the 5.33pm Manchester London Road-Marple stopping train near Reddish Vale. Note the elegant lines of the engine even when presenting a rear view. *Raymond Keeley*

*Above:* Class A5 No 69806 leaves London Road on the 12.10pm to Macclesfield on 25 October 1958. The rather dank gloomy day emphasising the problems that the engine seems to be suffering in the nether regions.
*Raymond Keeley*

*Below:* Class A5 No 69823 on the 7.48am London Road-Macclesfield on 14 July 1958. The train is leaving the higher of the short tunnels between Bredbury and Romiley, the lower being on the now lifted spur between the Stockport (Tiviot Dale) Woodley line and Romiley.
*Raymond Keeley*

*Below:* London Road station on 7 June 1958, Class A5 No 69815 on the 7.30am to Marple Rose Hill.
*Raymond Keeley*

*Above:* Class A5 No 69806 on the 1pm London Road–Hayfield arriving at Ashburys on 18 October 1958. *Raymond Keeley*

*Below:* Class A5 No 69817 with the 7.58am Manchester London Road-Marple shortly after leaving Bredbury on 14 June 1958. *Raymond Keeley*

*Above:* Marple on 22 September 1958. Class A5 No 69801, after the departure of the 6.07pm to Hayfield, proceeds to run round its train for the return to London Road at 6.10. The timings show that smart work was required by both station staff and engine crew. *Raymond Keeley*

*Below:* Class A5 No 69817 on the 7.30am London Road-Marple Rose Hill near Romiley. The train has travelled via Hyde and Woodley. The more direct line via Reddish and Bredbury passes beneath the arch on the left, joining the former shortly before entering Romiley station, on 12 September 1958. *Raymond Keeley*

*Above:* Class A5 No 69806 arriving at Marple Rose Hill with the 12.10pm London Road-Macclesfield on 24 May 1958. *Raymond Keeley*

*Below:* Smokebox ash being removed from the innards of Class A5 No 69826 on 22 May 1958 at Darlington Works; the handcart was a somewhat primitive handmaiden to this seamier side of steam locomotion. *Raymond Keeley*

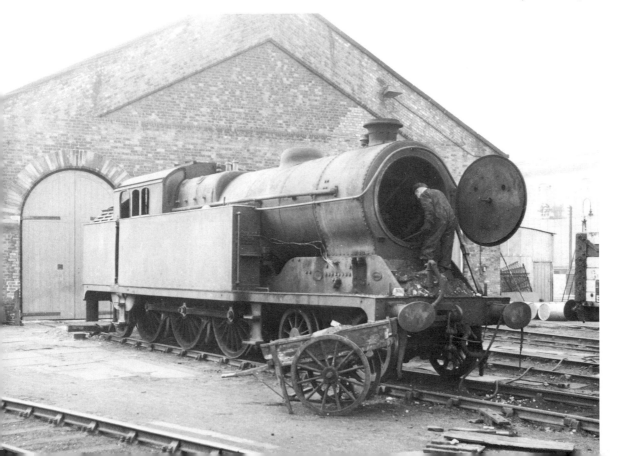

*Above:* Gorton on 28 July 1957. Class A5 No 69823 takes a welcome refresher. *Raymond Keeley*

*Below:* Class A8 No 69883 on Sunderland shed, 21 May 1958. The great bulk of these large tank engines is seen to advantage in this photograph, the human scale provided by courtesy of Alan Blencowe. *Raymond Keeley*

*Above:* Sunderland shed on 21 May 1958. Class A8 No 69862.   *Raymond Keeley*

*Below:* Darlington Works on 22 May 1958. End of the road for a couple of Pacific tanks. Awaiting scrapping are Class A5 No 69804 and A8 No 69865.   *Raymond Keeley*

# Freight Engine Multitude

In the 1950s the Eastern Regions of British Railways, which included the ex-LNER areas, were still dominated by the goods locomotives of the old pre-Grouping companies. An incredible situation when you consider the Grouping of those many highly individual railways into one was 30 years past.

An even more interesting aspect of this situation was the confining of certain types to definite areas, this applied even more to the freight engine classes than the passenger. Let us consider, for a moment, the position on the LNER in a little more detail. It is, for example extremely doubtful if a Great Eastern 0-6-0 ever strayed into the North Eastern stronghold of County Durham. Likewise I have never heard of any of the larger North Eastern 0-6-0s or 0-8-0s getting into East Anglia. As for a North British 0-6-0 crossing the border, well, it may have happened, though I cannot imagine they ever penetrated south of Newcastle. Tribal is the word that springs to mind, just imagine the raised eyebrows of disbelief if an enthusiast had found a North British 0-6-0 lurking in the depths of March or Cambridge sheds, where the Great Eastern, LNER Class J20 0-6-0s biggest and most powerful pre-Grouping 0-6-0s in Britain, reigned supreme. Likewise finding a Great Central, LNER Class J11 0-6-0, at Tyne Dock or Blaydon would have had the spotter of yesteryear rubbing his eyes wondering if the dank black gloom was causing hallucinations.

During the war I did occasionally find a North Eastern 0-8-0, LNER Class Q6, which had wandered far enough from home to climb over the Pennine gable on the Manchester-Sheffield line, though these were far from being the most rare visitors to venture into the darkness of the notorious Woodhead. One of the very few times I was able to record a North Eastern 4-6-0, LNER Class B15, was on 6 September 1942 in, of all places, Gorton depot. The B15s were few enough in number, even on their home ground by late 1942; to find one so far from home, in such an unexpected place, shows the thrill of discovery that sometimes came the way of the steam enthusiast. You never knew what lurked behind the next corner when you made your way up and down the massed locomotive lines of a dark Victorian steam shed.

The isolationism of some pre-Grouping sections of the LNER, which also happened on the Southern, and to a lesser extent on other grouped railways was, I believe, caused by what might be called, the size, power, competence, aspect of the locomotive stock inherited by the new company. Each of the groups was able to offer a well balanced range of motive power, designed to meet in detail the problems of each area. In this respect goods locomotives had the best of it, the companies grouped to form the LNER possessed between them what were arguably the finest fleets of heavy and medium goods locomotives in Britain.

By the time the Grouping had taken place the Great Central, Great Eastern, North Eastern, and North British railways had brought the development of that maid of all work, the 0-6-0 goods, to a full and final flowering in the classes which became LNER J11, J20, J27, J37, respectively. I am quite sure no greater quartet of 0-6-0s existed anywhere else in the country, significantly they all managed to get into the last decade of steam virtually intact. Gresley's own LNER Classes J38/39 didn't noticeably improve on performance of any of the above quartet. I have said these engines represented the final development of the type on their respective railways, it should be mentioned however, that in each case they were supported by medium or smaller 0-6-0s which were equally excellent for their size. The high standard of design in all these classes and the competent way they carried out the duties for which they were built made it unnecessary for the LNER to consider large scale replacement, even in the remote future. They were, in due course, augmented by modern types, though never supplanted. They continued for decades to do the jobs they were built for and rarely left their areas of origin.

East Anglia was, still is for that matter, a mainly agricultural area almost devoid of heavy industry, thus during the lifetime of the Great Eastern Railway nothing larger than the fine range of 0-6-0 classes were required to work the goods traffic. This situation lasted throughout the lifetime of the LNER, even in British Rail days it required little basic change. Since the Great Eastern was a natural for the 0-6-0 one could expect the group from that company to be good. In fact the engines which became LNER J15-20 were about the best balanced in terms of size and function ever to have existed.

The J15s were quite diminutive. I doubt if anything smaller, of the same type, with the possible exception of LNER Class J21 (ex-North Eastern), ventured so far into the last years of steam. They were a direct contrast to the mighty J20s, Britain's most powerful traditional style 0-6-0, despite the great size the J20s managed a balanced symmetrical appearance, unrivalled, I think, by any other 0-6-0 on the LNER. The boiler, though standard with those used on the B12 4-6-0s, did not seem oversize, if anything it served to underline the rangy confident stance of the locomotive.

Operating problems varied for all the railways mentioned but I doubt if greater contrast could be found than between the Great Eastern and North Eastern sections. On the latter railway heavy industry abounded especially in County Durham and Teeside, in the main it was solid heavy matter from the bowels of the earth, basically coal and iron ore, surely just about the heaviest material to move from A to B. The sort of weight seen today pounding our roads to rubble in the bulging juggernaut lorry loads of coal or stone. Yet the diesel or electric locomotive rolls loads vastly greater, smoothly, effortlessly along the railway.

In days of steam the story was different, six and eight coupled locomotives moved prodigious loads in trains, sometimes of great length. The burden of weight and movement clearly seen in columns of smoke and steam, sometimes at both head and tail of long, concertina like, rakes of small loose coupled wagons. A noble defiance of the most frustrating of the natural laws man grapples with — gravity!

The North Eastern had more than its share of this most spectacular facet of the steam locomotive in action. The central area of its activity, roughly bounded by County Durham, saw, in the railways' heyday, possibly the greatest concentration of heavyweight goods in Britain. Up to the turn of the century moderate sized 0-6-0s valiantly struggled with the loads, but the day of the big engine was about to dawn on the North Eastern. Significantly the first 4-6-0s (also among the first in this country) which were originally intended as express engines, became, in due course, more familiar as a mixed traffic unit. It was a role that successive types of 4-6-0 were unable to escape from, all, in their time, were associated with goods, fast goods or excursion work, it wasn't normally expected to see them otherwise engaged. Perhaps it was a subtle reflection of the basic nature of the North Eastern traffic, so magnificently camouflaged by the exploits of superb, flamboyant Atlantics.

In the summer of 1901 came the first of the heavy goods, the beginning of a family of 0-8-0s which, without doubt, became the most distinguished group of that wheel arrangement to exist in Britain. The North Eastern never went beyond the 0-8-0 in size, and time would prove they didn't need to. These engines became an elite, in a wheel arrangement that could lend itself more to clumsiness of appearance than elegance. They could also claim to be among the most powerful group of heavy freight locomotives built by any of the pre-Grouping railways — which is exactly as it should be!

The final development in this family of 0-8-0s, LNER Class Q7, were the most powerful and certainly the most strikingly handsome 0-8-0s ever seen in this country. The side view showed a locomotive unsurpassed in balance and symmetry, factors that sometimes are a problem in the absence of leading or trailing wheels to give a broad base to top weight. The boiler, imposingly large though not bloated, a feature spoiling the otherwise notable Lancashire and Yorkshire large boilered 0-8-0s, was pitched high enough to show space above the frames but not so high as to make it ungainly. This allowed for a line of attractively shaped boiler mountings which, being small, gave an increased sense of power. The boiler curve merged with the round topped firebox into the classic cab shape, a noticeable adornment to any North Eastern locomotive outline. A well raised running plate helped display a sturdy frame and four substantial driving wheels, the overhang of cab and smokebox were so neatly balanced as to give no sense of sag or heaviness. The whole was set off by outside cylinders which being slightly inclined gave uplift and thrust to the front end, where in some other 0-8-0s the feeling of being nose down was very pronounced.

The Q7s equal if not superior to most other big goods locomotives were probably only exceeded in power output by the BR 2-10-0s. Only 15 of these magnificent machines existed, and since they rarely worked outside a limited area in central County Durham, a pilgrimage to the Tyne Dock-Sunderland was required if you wished to see them. They survived well into the last decade of steam being just outlived by their smaller and older brethren, the LNER Class Q6 0-8-0s.

The Q6 was the real backbone of North Eastern goods 'heavies', by reason of numbers if nothing else, they dominated the Durham coalfields, and almost saw out the last few years of steam. Engines built new when the Q6s were old, had themselves gone for scrap while the older engines continued to do useful work. Though the Q7s impressed, their small numbers suggest the Q6s were well in control of most freight movement problems on the North Eastern. These engines, along with the B16s and others, are proof of the quality and know how behind the products of Darlington works. They also show that although the North Eastern may have been a rather provincial railway with roots in the coal seams, it had, in Vincent Raven, a brilliant far seeing railway engineer.

Towards the end of steam the charm for myself, and I suspect, the majority of enthusiasts, lay in the remoteness of many classes. In other words you really had to travel to East Anglia, Durham, Scotland, etc, if you wished to see certain types at work. Unlike today where the same types of diesel locomotive can be seen the length and breadth of the country. Yet even in the diesel age there have been the exceptions, the 'Westerns' and Deltics' for example, where the limiting to one main line or

section of the rail network, encouraged the pilgrimages of old, at least to some degree.

Because of these geographical limitations and the fact that many enthusiasts in the largely pre car era were limited in their movements, we tended to become familiar with railways and locomotives in confined areas, usually our home district. This in itself created the specialist photographers, and many illustrious names in the pre and postwar *Railway Magazine* who were associated with particular pre-Grouping areas are evidence of this.

The railway background of my life has always been dominated by the Manchester-Sheffield section of the old Great Central. The line over Woodhead, like other lines traversing the southern section of the long thick backbone dominating the trunk of the nation, posed a railway operating problem of huge proportions. Probing, climbing high into the hills to plunge deep into the bowels of summits unconquered.

During and after the last war I used this line frequently. They were the last great days of steam over Woodhead, always exciting, occasionally dramatic. I am sure no other line in the country offered such intensity of railway and locomotive interest, plus the most superb panoramas of hillside, valley and water. Passenger traffic, though always attracting the most glamorous of Great Central, and latterly LNER, motive power, was equalled in interest by the variety of freight engine types venturing into these hills.

Travelling west from Sheffield the fun really started at Penistone, the line twisting its way to find every advantage in the valley sides, ultimately to be confronted by a great landmass, and defeat, at Dunford the mountains triumphant as the train went to earth. A feature of this section of the line, and the corresponding western end of the tunnel, were the nose to tail goods trains. As your passenger train hauled by one of an almost infinite variety of motive power, at least in the 1940s laboured, with sense of great effort, towards, the summit, so the backward passing parade began. Just imagine a J11 wheezing mightily to assist an 04, perhaps 50 wagons away, then yards in front of the slowly nosing 04 the blunt tender backside of a Q6 in turn exerting indirect pressure towards a distant B8.

One of the most notable and unusual combinations I saw on this section, sometime in 1944, was a North Eastern B15 class 4-6-0 being assisted in the rear by none other than No 6165 *Valour*. This distinguished locomotive, then shedded at Gorton, being more familiar on passenger trains than banking a goods.

The discomfort of the dreaded single bores at Woodhead, nothing quite like them existed anywhere else, probably reached a peak during the war years of intensive freight and passenger movement. Riding through in a passenger train was bad enough, every window required to be tight shut, even so nostril tingling smoke and steam found a way in through the tiniest gaps in doors and corridor connections. To stand on the platform of Woodhead station watching a goods train, the engine well inside, being slowly engulfed by the west portal of the up line, was quite an experience. Smoke and steam squeezing its way through the unbelievably narrow gap between the sides and top of goods vans and the tunnel walls, drifted up the vertical rock face as if from a witch's couldron. At the rear, still some 15 or 20 wagons away, the guard in his van would be preparing for the ordeal ahead, with the prospect of 10min or more inside that nightmare hole. Conditions on the footplate, which I did once experience, were beyond relief. The drill seemed to be to tie a large moistened rag around nose and mouth then crouch or kneel as low as possible. The noise and general racket was almost undescribable. The thunder of the slow moving locomotive battering its exhaust against the low roof reverberated back as if through the very bones of the engine. Vibrations from heavy metal jarred the human limbs, all the senses assailed in one great cacophony. Ears cracked in the noise, sight lost in the obliterating dark, and above all the enveloping, cloying, warm muck, made vigorous effect to invade the lungs. It was a breed of iron men on iron horses who triumphed over such appalling conditions.

To take the title of this chapter, the legendary twin piercing of the Pennine gritstone knew a freight engine multitude, though none were more familiar in the last few decades of its life than Robinson's 2-8-0s. The name Woodhead is almost synonymous with the Class 04 and its variants. These engines, possibly J. G. Robinson's most important contribution to British Locomotive history, dominated the Great Central scene and were never seriously challenged as the best heavy goods locomotive regularly traversing this Pennine gable. The fact that this engine was chosen as one of the standard WD engines in World War I, and was still considered

good enough to go on active service in World War II, is a measure of its success. Both Gresley and Thompson in turn thought it a basically sound enough machine for modification, and even for extensive rebuilding in old age.

Unlike some modern classes of freight engine, the Stanier 2-8-0s and BR 2-10-0s for example, I cannot possibly imagine the 04 was ever used on relatively fast passenger service in this country. However it did happen overseas and it has always been a matter of great personal satisfaction that I made at least one long journey across Egypt behind one. It was a night trip crossing the Nile delta — the beating heart of this vast country — from near Suez to Alexandria, in the first leg of the long trek back to Britain and demob. How well I remember that open wooden carriage, baking hot, even though the windows were without glass. All the marvellous, pungent smells and sounds of this unique country carried on the warm night air to pervade the senses, like a farewell reminder of an extraordinary experience, only to come our way, at least the majority of us, once in a lifetime. There are other memories too, of kitbags clutched between the legs, heads dozing on other belongings gathered inside widespread arms — protection against thieves who, with unbelievable stealth, stalked the night and the trains to seize what they could from under your nose.

Ironically it wasn't until arrival at Alexandria next morning that I discovered vintage Great Central steam at the head of the train. I had been conscious of fast and lively running on the Ismailia-Benha section, but as previous experience on the same section behind Egyptian State Railway Atlantics had produced very fast running, it didn't seem unusual. Perhaps drivers were less inhibited about the speed eight coupled wheels should revolve than might be the case on the engines' home ground.

Maybe I will be challenged if I use the word beauty in connection with the 04s. How can anything so rugged, 'built like a battleship' might be the phrase, look beautiful? I hope the photograph of No 63686 at London Road will help to make the point. For me this has always been 'beauty in repose', getting the right angle was perhaps that stroke of luck with which fortune sometimes favours the photographer. It is probably hard to imagine from the appearance of the gentle looking creature in the photograph that this is the engine for whom the Pennine gable held no terrors, which reigned unchallenged for heavy goods work on the Great Central section almost at the end of steam.

Except for one or two preserved examples, these great fleets of ironclad steam breathing mastodons have, like the huge battleships with which they were contemporary, gone the way of most things man creates from inanimate matter. To be replaced, perhaps with some of that same matter now rejuvenated, by something superior in performance, ease of handling and comfort for the footplate staff. But inferior in terms of the satisfaction some men found in coaxing, cajoling, nursing this most lifelike and emotive of man's creations. To say nothing of the joy many of us found in this passing parade of life.

*Above right:* **Woodley Junction c1959. Class O4/8 coming off the Stockport (Tiviot Dale) line with a freight train. Line to the left is for Romiley, now traversed regularly by the steam specials that operate between Guide Bridge and Sheffield. The O4/8 was one of the several variants of the Robinson design, in this case with a Thompson O1 type boiler and cab but retaining original cylinders, frames etc.** *Raymond Keeley*

*Below right:* **Manchester London Road station on 3 August 1957. Class O4/1 No 63686. The engine, on route to Gorton, is standing on the MSJ&A side of the station, and awaits clearance to cross London Midland metals to the Eastern Region side.** *Raymond Keeley*

*Below:* **Mexborough depot on 10 May 1959. Class O4/1 Nos 63658 and 63599. Both engines remain substantially as built, thus showing, despite the slightly battered look in places, the classic good looks of the Robinson locomotive, an attribute of all his designs, even the heavy freight engine.** *Raymond Keeley*

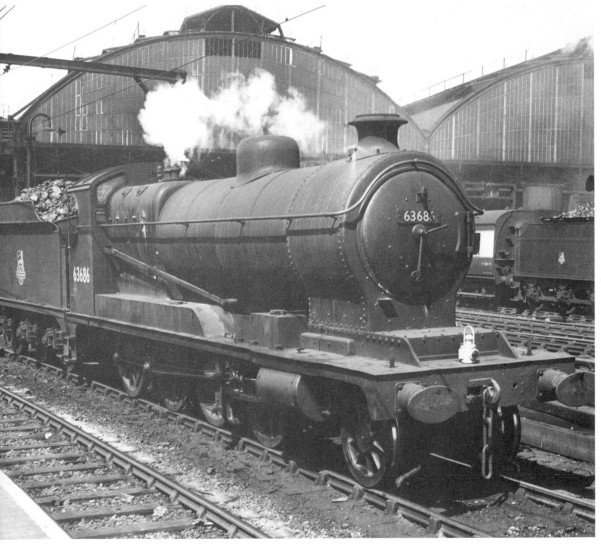

*Left:* Class O4/8 No 63895 running light near Reddish Vale on 7 July 1958. *Raymond Keeley*

*Below:* Woodhouse station on 17 September 1958. Class O4/3 No 63842 passing to the rear of the station on the down slow line. At this station both up and down slow lines pass round the outside of platforms both of which face on to the up and down fast lines making them island platforms but with a difference. The engine classification of O4/3 shows that although the basic Robinson design it was in fact built during World War 1 for the ROD. The engine certainly enjoyed a long life since withdrawal did not take place until 1965. *Raymond Keeley*

*Above:* Class O4/8 No 63731 passing through Manchester Exchange station with an Ardwick-Ordsall Lane transfer freight on 24 September 1960. *Raymond Keeley*

*Centre right:* One of Sir Vincent Raven's long lived heavy goods 0-8-0s, Class Q6 No 63415 stands alongside the coaling stage at West Hartlepool depot on 21 May 1958. Most of this class had a half century of working life behind them before they went for scrap. *Raymond Keeley*

*Below right:* West Hartlepool again on 21 May 1958. One of the WD Austerity 2-8-0s stands alongside a Class Q6 0-8-0 No 63414. *Raymond Keeley*

*Left:* Darlington shed on 21 May 1958. Class Q6 No 63405 ex-works, gleams in the low evening sunshine. *Raymond Keeley*

*Centre left:* Tyne Dock shed on 30 May 1962. Class Q7 0-8-0 No 63462 receives a little of that attention so vital to the well being of any steam locomotive. *Alan Blencowe*

*Below:* Blaydon shed on 20 May 1958. Q7s Nos 63464 and 63462 and J72 0-6-0T No 69023. *Alan Blencowe*

*Above right:* Doncaster station on 10 June 1959. Class J6 0-6-0 No 64241. The J6s were the ultimate development of the Great Northern 0-6-0, but since they were designed by Gresley his later J39 class for the LNER might well be considered the real final development. *Raymond Keeley*

*Below right:* Blaydon shed on 20 May 1958. Class Q7 63472, Britain's biggest and most handsome 0-8-0. *Alan Blencowe*

*Above:* The ultimate in size, North British 0-6-0. Class J37 No 64624, carrying a St Margaret's shed plate (64A), running up to the Forth Bridge through North Queensferry on 30 May 1963. Alan Blencowe's picture admirably captures the towering appearance of these large 0-6-0s. *Alan Blencowe*

*Left:* West Hartlepool shed on 21 May 1958. Class J26 0-6-0 No 65747. The J26s along with the almost identical J27s that followed, represented another ultimate in size being the largest 0-6-0s designed for the North Eastern Railway, and among the largest in Britain. Like others of the class No 65747 had an incredibly long life of 58 years. *Raymond Keeley*

*Above right:* Class J11 0-6-0 No 64331 simmering on the ash pit Woodford shed on 25 August 1955. Apart from goods workings the Woodford engines were widely used on local passenger trains to Leicester and Banbury. *Alan Blencowe*

*Centre right:* Gresley's standard 0-6-0 Class J39. This one, No 64899, is seen in sunshine and shadow at Carlisle Canal shed on 30 August 1961. *Alan Blencowe*

*Below:* Sages Lane Crossing (north of Peterborough) on 24 September 1955. Class J39 No 64896 with an up goods on ex-Midland lines (Peterborough-Leicester via Stamford). *Alan Blencowe*

*Above:* Class J17 No 65538 on an up 'pickup' goods at Chatteris on 22 October 1956. The J17 class 0-6-0s designed by Holden for the Great Eastern Railway was another long lived class. No 65538 built in 1901 lasted until 1959 — almost 60 years of service. *Alan Blencowe*

*Below:* Cambridge shed on 16 June 1957, Class J17 No 65508. The grime of the average steam shed is well emphasised in this photograph. *Alan Blencowe*